THE CIVIL WAR
AND THE WARS OF THE NINETEENTH CENTURY

THE CIVIL WAR
AND THE WARS OF THE NINETEENTH CENTURY

BRIAN HOLDEN REID

Series Editor, John Keegan

Smithsonian Books

Collins

An Imprint of HarperCollinsPublishers

To the memory of my father, Robert Holden Reid (1918–98)

Text © Brian Holden Reid, 1999
Design and layout © Cassell
The picture credits on p. 240 constitute an extension to this copyright page.
The American Civil War chronology on pp. 10–12 is reproduced by kind
permission of Peter Parish, *The American Civil War* (Eyre & Spottiswoode, 1975).
First published in Great Britain, 1999
Reprinted 2000
UK paperback edition 2002
U.S. paperback edition 2006

HarperCollins books may be purchased for educational, business, or sales
promotional use. For information, please write: Special Markets Department,
HarperCollins Publishers, 10 East 53rd Street, New York, NY 10022.

Published 2006 in the United States of America by Smithsonian Books
In association with Cassell
Wellington House, 125 Strand
London, WC2R 0BB

Library of Congress Cataloging-in-publication data has been applied for.
ISBN-10: 0-06-085120-1
ISBN-13: 978-0-06-085120-0

Manufactured in Spain, not at government expense

Title Page: *Three Union officers pose before a Napoleon cannon in 1862.*

Overleaf: *Few roofs have survived. The centre of Richmond, Virginia, after the
Confederate surrender in April 1865. Covered wagons can be seen entering the
devastation on the left.*

Acknowledgements

THIS IS A BRIEF book covering a series of major, tumultuous events. My prime concern has been to present a clear account of what actually happened during the significant wars of the mid nineteenth century, a period that witnessed the full impact of the Industrial Revolution on warfare. A shortage of space has prevented me from discussing the huge array of issues arising from the social and political dimensions of strategy, yet I have selected one aspect that particularly interests me, namely the technique of higher command and the pressures that technological change imposed upon it.

I am grateful to a number of people who have helped with the publication of this book. First and foremost is my general editor, John Keegan, whose friendship and support I greatly value. I am also much indebted, and the promissory notes are now building up over many years, to the late Peter J. Parish who read the entire typescript with his usual critical care and greatly improved it. I am also grateful to my colleague, Professor Andrew Lambert, for commenting on the chapter on the Crimean War. I have also learned much about the Franco-Prussian War from Professor Richard Holmes. Our innumerable visits together to the battlefields of Lorraine literally opened up for me a new vista on the tangled woodland of war. I am also obliged to Michael Knight for his serenity and good humour during a trying time. At Orion, I am beholden to Judith Flanders for sympathetic editorial guidance, to Penny Gardiner for all her hard work in co-ordinating the text, illustrations and maps, and to Malcolm Swanston for his skill in drawing them. As with two of my earlier books, I have had the great good fortune to enjoy the secretarial services of Penny Eldridge, who has produced a typescript of an exemplary standard.

The gestation of this book has been overshadowed by sudden and unexpected bereavement. It is dedicated to the one whose opinion I would have preferred to have heard first.

BRIAN HOLDEN REID
King's College London

Contents

KEY TO MAPS

Military units–types

⊠ infantry

◣ cavalry

Military units–size

army

ROSECRANS

XXX
▭ corps

XX
▭ division

elts elements of unit

GD grand division

Military unit colours

Union

Confederate

phase 1 phase 2

Military movements

➤ attack

➥ retreat

General military symbols

⚔ site of battle

☆ fort

ᒫᒧᒫ fortifications

〜 seige line

● ● ● defensive position

⊹ field gun

Geographical symbols

urban area

urban area (3D maps)

——— road

═══ road (larger scale maps)

railway

—— river

- - - seasonal river

⊔⊔⊔ canal

—— border

⋈ bridge

⋈ ford

Map list

Chronology

CRIMEAN WAR (1854-6)

1853	
4 Oct	Opening of Russo-Turkish War.
23 Oct	Turks cross the Danube into the Russian-held Principalities of Moldavia and Wallachia.
30 Nov	Defeat of wooden Turkish fleet by Russian steam battle-ships at Sinope.

1854	
Jan	British and French warships sail into the Black Sea.
12 Jan	Great Britain and France sign treaties of alliance with Turkey, guaranteeing the integrity of the Ottoman Empire.
23 Jan	Russian troops cross Danube into East Bulgaria and besiege Silistria.
23 Jan	Great Britain and France declare war on Russia.
17 Jul	Anglo-French war council decides to invade Crimea and besiege Sevastopol.
17–19 Sep	53,000 Anglo-French troops land at Evpatoria, 40 miles north of Sevastopol, and advance south.
20 Sep	Russians defeated at the battle of Alma.
17 Oct	Allies occupy Balaclava and begin to bombard Sevastopol.
25 Oct	Battle of Balaclava, concluding with the 'Charge of the Light Brigade'.
4 Nov	Battle of Inkerman.

1855	
18 Jan	Death of Tsar Nicholas I.
9 Apr	Massive Allied bombardment of Sevastopol.
4–26 May	Allies eventually occupy Kerch. General Jean-Jacques Pélissier appointed French commander.

6 Jun	Anglo-French assault on Mamelon, Malakoff and the Redan fails.
17–18 Jun	Second Allied assault on Russian defences fails.
28 Jun	Death of Raglan. He is replaced by James Simpson.
15 Aug	Failure of Russian counter-attack.
5–8 Sep	Preliminary bombardment of Sevastopol.
8 Sep	French take the Malakoff and (despite a British repulse) the Redan falls. Menshikov evacuates Sevastopol.
28 Dec	The Austrian 'ultimatum' is presented to Russia embodying the French peace terms.

1856

16 Jan	Tsar Alexander II accepts the terms of the Austrian 'ultimatum'.
1 Feb	Peace preliminaries signed.
25 Feb	Congress of Paris opens.
30 Mar	Treaty of Paris.
15 Apr	The Three Power Alliance (Great Britain, France and Austria) created to safeguard Crimean settlement.

CIVIL WAR (1861–5)

1860

6 Nov	Abraham Lincoln elected president.

1861

4 Mar	Inauguration of Abraham Lincoln as president.
29 Mar	Lincoln orders preparation of Fort Sumter relief expedition.
12–13 Apr	Bombardment and surrender of Fort Sumter.
15 Apr	Lincoln declares state of insurrection and calls for 75,000 militia.
19 Apr	Lincoln proclaims blockade of Southern coast.
Jun–Jul	Political and military moves to secure Union control of West Virginia.
21 Jul	Confederate victory at First Manassas (or Bull Run).

27 Jul	McClellan takes command of Union forces around Washington.
10 Aug	Confederate victory at Wilson's Creek, Missouri.
29 Aug	Union success at Hatteras Inlet, on North Carolina coast.
1 Nov	McClellan becomes general-in-chief of all Union armies.
7 Nov	Union capture of Port Royal on South Carolina coast.
20 Dec	Creation of Joint Committee on the Conduct of the War.

1862

15 Jan	Stanton becomes secretary of war.
6 Feb	Union capture of Fort Henry on Tennessee river.
8 Feb	Union success at Roanoke Island, North Carolina.
16 Feb	Confederates surrender Fort Donelson to Grant.
25 Feb	Confederate evacuation of Nashville.
7–8 Mar	Union victory at Pea Ridge (or Elkhorn Tavern), Arkansas.
8–9 Mar	*Virginia* v. *Monitor* in Hampton Roads.
17 Mar–2 Apr	Movement of McClellan's army to James Peninsula.
5–4 Apr	McClellan besieges Yorktown.
6–7 Apr	Grant turns near-defeat into Union victory at Shiloh.
24–5 Apr	New Orleans falls to Admiral Farragut.
8–9 May	Jackson's Shenandoah Valley campaign.
31 May–1 Jun	Battle of Seven Pines or Fair Oaks near Richmond. Lee takes command of Army of Northern Virginia.
6 Jun	Confederate evacuation of Memphis.
26 Jun	Creation of Army of Virginia under John Pope.
26 Jun–2 Jul	Lee drives McClellan back from Richmond in Seven Days battles.
June–July	Failure of Union naval operations against Vicksburg.
11 Jul	Halleck appointed general-in-chief of Union armies.
17 Jul	Second Confiscation Act.
22 Jul	Lincoln reads draft Emancipation Proclamation to Cabinet.
3 Aug	Decision to evacuate McClellan's army from peninsula.

27–8 Aug	Beginning of Confederate invasion of Kentucky.
29–30 Aug	Confederate victory at Second Manassas (or Bull Run).
2 Sep	McClellan in command of defence of Washington.
4–6 Sep	Lee invades Maryland.
17 Sep	Battle of Antietam followed by Lee's withdrawal into Virginia.
19 Sep	Union defensive victory at Iuka, Mississippi.
22 Sep	First Emancipation Proclamation.
3–4 Oct	Union defensive victory at Corinth, Mississippi.
8 Oct	Battle of Perryville, Kentucky, followed by retreat of Bragg's Confederate army.
7 Nov	McClellan dismissed. Burnside assumes command of Army of the Potomac.
Nov–Dec	Failure of Grant's overland advance towards Vicksburg.
13 Dec	Lee crushes Burnside at Fredericksburg.
16–20 Dec	Cabinet crisis. Lincoln retains both Seward and Chase.
27–9 Dec	Sherman defeated at Chickasaw Bluffs, near Vicksburg.
31 Dec–3 Jan	Battle of Murfreesboro (or Stones river), followed by Bragg's withdrawal.

1863

1 Jan	Second Emancipation Proclamation
25 Jan	Burnside replaced by Hooker as commander of Army of the Potomac.
Feb–Apr	Grant's abortive attempts to find back door to Vicksburg.
16–17 Apr	Porter's ships run past the Vicksburg batteries.
30 Apr–6 May	Lee routs Hooker at Chancellorsville.
1–18 May	Grant's successful campaign in Mississippi. Pemberton trapped in Vicksburg.
10 May	Death of 'Stonewall' Jackson.
3 Jun	Start of Lee's advance north.
26–7 Jun	Rosecrans manoeuvres Confederates under Bragg back towards Chattanooga.
28 Jun	Hooker replaced by Meade as commander of Army of the Potomac.

1–3 Jul	Union victory at Gettysburg.
4 Jul	Vicksburg surrenders to Grant.
8 Jul	Confederates surrender Port Hudson, on Mississippi.
13–14 Jul	Lee retreats across Potomac into Virginia.
20 Jul	Rosecrans begins movement to south of Chattanooga.
19–20 Sep	Rosecrans defeated by Bragg at Chickamauga.
17 Oct	Grant becomes overall Union commander in West.
28 Oct	Relief of Union forces besieged in Chattanooga.
24–5 Oct	Union victory at Chattanooga.

1864

8 Mar	Union defeat at Mansfield (or Sabine Cross Roads), Louisiana, leads to abandonment of Red river expedition.
9 Mar	Grant becomes general-in-chief.
12 Mar	Forrest captures Fort Pillow, Tennessee; massacre of black troops.
4 May	Start of major Union offensive in Virginia and Georgia.
5–6 May	Battle of the Wilderness.
8–21 May	Battles at Spotsylvania Court House.
25–9 May	Battle between Sherman and Joseph E. Johnston around New Hope Church, Georgia.
1–3 Jun	Battle of Cold Harbor.
14–16 Jun	Grant's army moves south of James river.
15–18 Jun	Failure of attacks of Petersburg; beginning of nine-month siege.
27 Jun	Sherman defeated at Kennesaw Mountain.
11 Jul	Confederate force led by Jubal A. Early reaches outskirts of Washington.
17 Jul	Hood replaces Johnston as Confederate commander at Atlanta.
20–28 Jul	Battles around Atlanta.
30 Jul	Union failure at battle of the 'crater', near Petersburg.
2 Sep	Sherman captures Atlanta.
19–22 Sep	Sheridan's victories at Opequon Creek and Fisher's Hill, in Shenandoah Valley.

23 Sep	Union victory over Sterling Price at Westport, Missouri, ends major fighting west of Mississippi.
8 Nov	Lincoln re-elected president.
15–16 Nov	Start of Sherman's march from Atlanta to the sea.
30 Nov	Confederates under Hood defeated at Franklin, Tennessee.
15–16 Dec	Hood's Confederates crushed by Thomas at Nashville.
21 Dec	Savannah falls to Sherman.

1865

15 Jan	Union forces capture Fort Fisher, North Carolina.
31 Jan	Congress passes Thirteenth Amendment, abolishing slavery.
1 Feb	Start of Sherman's march through the Carolinas.
17 Feb	Burning of Columbia, South Carolina. Confederates evacuate Charleston.
4 Mar	Lincoln's second inauguration.
21–3 Mar	Completion of Sherman's march. Junction with Schofield's forces in North Carolina.
30–31 Mar	Beginning of Grant's final assault in Virginia.
2 Apr	Fall of Petersburg.
3 Apr	Fall of Richmond.
9 Apr	Lee surrenders to Grant at Appomattox Court House.
14–15 Apr	Lincoln shot by John Wilkes Booth, dies next morning.
26 Apr	Joseph E. Johnston surrenders in North Carolina.
26 May	Surrender of Kirby Smith in trans-Mississippi region brings war formally to an end.

GERMAN WARS OF UNIFICATION (1864, 1866, 1870–71)

1864

21 Jan	Austro-Prussian forces invade Holstein.
18 Apr	Fall of Dybbøl; most of Jutland occupied by Austrians and Prussians.

9 May	Denmark defeats Austrian fleet at the battle of Heligoland.
20 Jul	Armistice signed.
30 Oct	Denmark cedes Schleswig and Holstein to Prussia and Austria by the Treaty of Vienna.

1866

8 Apr	Alliance signed between Prussia and Italy in Berlin and Florence.
21 Apr	Austrian mobilization begins.
4, 7 May	Prussian mobilization begins.
15 Jun	Prussian forces invade Saxony, Hanover and Hesse.
17–18 Jun	Austro-Prussian War opens.
20 Jun	Italy declares war on Austria.
23–6 Jun	Prussian First and Second Armies advance into Bohemia.
24 Jun	Austrian victory over the Italians at Custozza.
27 Jun	Austrian victory at Trautenau.
29 Jun	Prussian successes at Burkersdorf, Rudersdorf and Skalice; seizure of Jicin.
1 Jul	Benedek withdraws to Königgrätz.
2 Jul	Moltke changes his plan and orders Second Army to advance on Chlum.
3 Jul	Austrians defeated at the battle of Königgrätz.
10 Jul	Benedek withdraws to Olmütz.
26 Jul	Austria sues for peace.
Aug	Treaty of Prague: Austria paid an indemnity of 30m florins ($405m) to Prussia and agreed to Prussia's annexation of Schleswig– Holstein, Hanover, Hesse–Kassel, Nassau and Frankfurt; Prussia also gained indirect control of other territories by organizing the North German Confederation.
3 Oct	Treaty of Vienna: Venetia transferred to Italy.

1868

Sep	Queen Isabella driven from the Spanish throne.

1869
Apr	Hohenzollern candidacy to Spanish throne first discussed.

1870
22 Apr	Offer of Spanish throne turned down by Leopold, Prince of Hohenzollern-Sigmaringen.
2 Jul	News of Leopold's candidacy angers French press.
6 Jul	French declaration issued stating that a Prussian candidate on the Spanish throne would be against the interests and honour of France.
13 Jul	Ems Telegram.
15–19 Jul	France decides on war with Prussia.
6 Aug	Battles of Spicheren and Worth.
16 Aug	Battles of Vionville and Mars-la-Tour.
18 Aug	Battles of Rezonville-Gravelotte-St Privat; Bazaine withdraws into the fortress of Metz.
26, 31 Aug	Bazaine fails to break out from Metz.
1–3 Sep	Surrender of Sedan: Napoleon III, 104,000 soldiers and 419 cannon captured by Prussians.
4 Sep	Overthrow of Second Empire; the Third Republic proclaimed.
20 Sep	First Prussian troops invade Paris.
29 Oct	Bazaine surrenders Metz.

1871
5 Jan	Bombardment of Paris begins.
18 Jan	William I proclaimed German Emperor in the Hall of Mirrors at Versailles.
19 Jan	French garrison of Paris asks for an armistice.
28 Jan	Armistice comes into force; Franco-Prussian War ends.
26 Feb	Peace preliminaries agreed.
3 Mar	Peace preliminaries ratified at the Treaty of Frankfurt. France is required to pay an indemnity of 5 billion francs and lost Alsace and one third of Lorraine.

War and Industrialization

'Professor' Thaddeus S. Lowe and his balloon
Intrepid. Lowe is seated on the ground in the pith
helmet writing an intelligence report for George B.
McClellan during the Peninsular Campaign in the
summer of 1862. By June he had two yellow-coloured
balloons observing Confederate troop movements.
They remained tied to the ground, and when Lowe
had something to report, the balloon was pulled
earthwards. The telegraph operator is waiting to send
Lowe's message. Due to bad luck, Lowe failed to get
his balloons up at the crucial moment, and it was
difficult to see through the thick woods. In historian
Stephen Sears's opinion, balloons 'brought very little
real enlightenment' to the Union command.

War and Industrialization

THIS BOOK IS A short comparative history. It is a survey of three wars, the Crimean War (1854–6), the American Civil War (1861–5) and the German Wars of Unification (1864, 1866, 1870–71). As all levels of human intercourse are mainly about power, the influence of politics on war will be an important theme in the pages that follow. Sir Herbert Butterfield, in his book *Man on His Past* (1955), quotes Schlozer, a German eighteenth-century historian, who was of the opinion that 'History without politics is mere monkish chronicles'. These three wars (or groups of wars) were fought more than 4,000 miles apart; yet the first and third were brought about by changes in the balance of power, and the second was fought to prevent (among other things) a balance of power being created in North America. The focus will, therefore, be on the grand strategy, military strategy and operations during this period – that compound of elements that often leads to a combustible shift in the relations between nation states. However, the book takes a different tack from many comparable surveys of the mid nineteenth century. In the writings of Eric Hobsbawm, for instance – and most notably in his distinguished trilogy on nineteenth-century civilization – the United States is treated as rather marginal to European affairs. In this book such an approach has been reversed. American history has been placed right at the centre of these tumultuous events. This is right and proper, not just because the American Civil War was the greatest struggle of the nineteenth century – the most destructive conflict between the Napoleonic Wars (1798–1815) and the 'First World War (1914–18) – but because Europeans are inclined to forget that the rise of the United States to world power is the greatest historical event of the nineteenth century.

While the temptation to treat the United States as a kind of appendage to the perpetual struggle over the European balance of power must be resisted, it needs to be understood that American influence on world affairs was still limited. It is because the North brought the Civil War to a victorious conclusion and thus prevented the disintegration of the United States into two (or perhaps four) competing republics, that the massive spread of American power and culture was able to occur in the twentieth century. The general historical importance of the events of 1861–5, combined with the war's intrinsic military significance, more than justifies devoting greater attention to this conflict than to the other wars covered in this book.

American statesmen realized after independence was gained from Britain in 1783 that American diplomatic influence, compared with that of the great European powers, carried little weight. George Washington rationalized a policy of disengagement from Europe in his famous 'Farewell Address' (1796). His precepts guided American foreign relations throughout the nineteenth century. He counselled avoiding alliances with more powerful European countries while building up American wealth by concentrating on internal development. Thomas Jefferson christened this policy when he urged the avoidance of 'entangling alliances'. It was ironic that the pursuit of this policy would unleash the quarrels that resulted in the American Civil War. That is, American domestic expansion stimulated social tensions that led to war. In 1862 European powers tottered briefly on the precipice of intervening to aid the South in its struggle for independence. The

Abraham Lincoln, sixteenth President of the United States. 'Well boys,' he said to reporters after his election, 'your problems are over, mine are about to begin.' He did not exaggerate. 'I believe,' he complained in 1863, 'I feel trouble in the air before it comes.'

American presidents who followed Washington aimed to prevent European influence from spreading to North America. They believed that new European colonies would bring in their train all the covetous wickedness of the European balance of power, with its resultant bloodshed, destruction and suffering. President James Monroe in his famous 'doctrine', which was enunciated in his message to Congress in December 1823, claimed that the western hemisphere was a separate system from the 'Old World'. Europeans were warned that 'any attempt on their part to extend their system to any portion of this hemisphere' would be regarded as 'dangerous to our peace and safety'.

American isolation, especially when extended to embrace the entire western hemisphere, is really an attitude of mind towards Europe. Isolation involves keeping the United States distinct from and free of the glutinous clutches of the European balance of power. As American wealth and power grew, so the United States was able to enforce an *imbalance of power* over, first of all, North America and eventually over Latin America as well. With few threats to American security, there was little need for large and expensive armed forces.

The fruit of this imbalance was total security and a gradual accumulation of American power that would one day overshadow the European monarchies. The young Abraham Lincoln, in his first major public address at the Lyceum in Springfield, Illinois, in 1838, asserted that the United States was too big to be invaded successfully. 'All the armies of Europe, Asia and Africa combined,' he claimed, '… with a Bonaparte as a commander, could not by force take a drink from the Ohio.' Yet the heart of the matter lay in the perpetual and inviolate character of the federal Union. So long as this continued, the growing imbalance could be preserved. If it fractured, then something akin to a European balance of power would spread to North America, with intervention by European powers, bringing with them, like the plague, their wars, strife and oppression of liberties. It is perhaps the supreme irony that American internal development continued without interruption during this period because of the naval predominance of Great Britain.

The other important theme of this book is the relationship between war, national identity and the balance of power. There exists a ceaseless dance of shifting diplomatic and strategic relationships that involves all states, however remote or reluctant, as they seek to advance their interests and occupy the best tables around the ballroom floor. New partners are taken up, others discarded; old dalliances long forgotten have a habit of being resumed. One of the most important ways in which interests could be extended or protected was maritime power. Great Britain's desire to safeguard a balance of power in Europe that was not prejudicial to its interests and its sea lines of communication with its Empire rested on its naval supremacy. As a term, however, the 'balance of power' is a misnomer. What powers strive to gain is a preponderance of power in their favour rather than an exact balance. Martin Wight, in his book *Power Politics* (1978), expounds the concept of the *dominant power*. This is a power 'that can measure strength against all rivals combined'. Such potency had already been secured by the Royal Navy during the nineteenth century and it would be put to use during the Crimean War. British imperial policy during the eighteenth century had led to Great Britain becoming the dominant power in North America. Britain's power was shattered by the American Revolution (1775–83). Although Canada remained a British colony, the United States believed itself to be Britain's heir as the dominant power in the western hemisphere. For Europeans, in contrast, the events most pregnant with war and upheaval were the sequence of three wars that led to German unification. On two occasions in the first half of the twentieth century, Germany has sought to gain for itself a position as the world's dominant power by the employment of naked military force that the two maritime powers, Great Britain and the United States, have eschewed. These three wars, then, have had a major – if not pivotal – influence on the history of the western world. How were they fought?

The century after the Congress of Vienna (1814–15) did not witness a war involving all the European powers. Yet it was a period in which all powers prepared for war. The predominant influence on the calculations of soldiers and statesmen was the Industrial Revolution. Historians have questioned whether the Industrial Revolution actually occurred in any meaningful, dramatic sense; but what is undeniable is that warfare between 1815 and 1875 was transformed in scale, impact and destructiveness. The last stages of the Napoleonic wars revealed strong hints of a greater intensity in the conduct of war, especially during the climactic campaign of 1813 in Germany culminating in the 'battle of the Nations' at Leipzig. Nevertheless, the tactical pattern of Napoleonic warfare was an exact one. The infantry attacked with their bayonets, supported by the cavalry and artillery, and drove the enemy's infantry from the battlefield. An articulated system of self-supporting corps dispersed during the campaign's preliminary manoeuvres and concentrated on the battlefield. The enemy's flanks were then attacked in an attempt to find his rear – the most vulnerable point of any army – a process termed envelopment. Elements of Napoleonic warfare have persisted, even to this day, yet social and technological changes have brought great strain to bear on it. Many commanders were confused and learned (like Napoleon III) that armies were not as easy to command as they thought. However, the essential strength of the Napoleonic legacy was shown by the successful envelopments carried out by the Austrian general, Count Radetzky, against the Sardinians in northern Italy in 1849. Other generals would not always be so successful.

Observers would note that, over the twenty years following the end of the Napoleonic Wars in 1815, cavalry was losing its influence on the battlefield itself, though not off it. Artillery seemed to be losing its potency, too. It could no longer unlimber within 300 yards of the infantry and open fire with impunity, even though shrapnel was available – a destructive weapon against infantry because the projectile shattered in their midst when triggered by a time fuse. A general tendency could be discerned which heralded the reduction in effectiveness of shock weapons – those rammed home at close quarters by physical force.

These developments could be explained largely by the impact of industrialization on war. Machines started to exert their tenacious grip over man's activities. Factories displaced the craftsmen spawned by cottage industries. Economies of scale were possible allowing the creation of a production line and levels of manufacture commensurate with the ability to produce. The craftsman supported the production line, not the other way round. Mass production, in turn, demanded purchasing power, and an economic and financial system that could create it. A demand for labour and its concentration in industrial centres stimulated a growth in population which added to the human as well as material stock of war-making resources available. Between 1815 and 1850 German coal and lignite production rose from 1.2 to 9.2 million tonnes; pig-iron production grew from 85,000 tonnes in 1823 to 1 million in 1867. Between 1865 and 1879 German steel production quadrupled. Northern production of pig-iron during the American Civil War reached a peak of 1,136 thousand 'long tons' in 1864. The development of standardized machine tools permitted the production of huge numbers of identical and interchangeable parts which, in turn, allowed the repair and replacement of huge numbers of weapons. Increasingly, such resources were rationalized and eventually reorganized, as the bureaucratic methods necessary to run an industrial economy were extended to armies.

Consequently, wars fought during the nineteenth century became more national. Nation states of the mid nineteenth century were self-confident, commercially vital, subject to industrial expansion, and enjoyed free trade within their borders. They were also increasingly influenced by an urban, middle-class outlook, conveniently placed under the generic heading of 'liberalism'. Such citizens tended to be patriotic and restless – confident and aggressive if not invariably 'progressive'. Their well-educated curiosity bred a fascination with Napoleon, war and revolution. After 1815 the cult of Napoleon spread to the United States. Napoleon's brother, Joseph Bonaparte, had lived in splendour near Bordentown, New Jersey. Marshal Grouchy, whom many blamed for Napoleon's defeat at Waterloo, was a resident of Philadelphia. But throughout the West, public opinion was engaged and excited by martial events; it was prone to see war in rather sentimental terms as a glamorous adventure replete with romantic heroes. Andrew Jackson might adopt some Napoleonic airs and be accused by his enemies of regal ambitions, but it was in European politics that the military adventurer struck the deepest chord. The emperor Napoleon III shamelessly exploited the memory of his uncle. Military heroes were revered in even more prosaic societies. The Duke of Wellington was a respectable version in Britain, and Strauss composed his 'Radetzky March' in honour of the Austrian general to the delight of Vienna society.

Alterations in the character of war on which these social forces fed was influenced by the technology available. Science and technology lie at the very core of industrialization because they permit the perfection of theoretical design. Technology had an impact in three broad areas: in weaponry, strategic movement and organization.

The most significant development in weaponry was the cylindro-conoidal bullet. The original inventor was Captain Norton, who in 1823 succeeded in developing a bullet which expanded to seal the bore of a rifle. In 1836 William Greener inserted a conoidal wooden plug into the base of the bullet, and it was this design that the Frenchman C. E. Minié adapted into the Minié bullet. Although the British Ordnance Department rejected the first designs, in 1851 the Minié bullet was issued to the British Army (Minié having been paid £20,000 for the

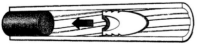

THE MINIÉ PRINCIPLE
The bullet is rammed back on the charge. It explodes, sending the bullet spiralling down the barrel, expanding as it goes and, gripped by the grooves in a gas-tight fit, the bullet hurtles towards its target.

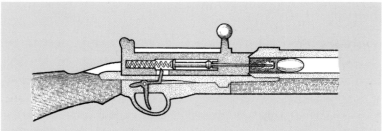

The Dreyse mechanism

The bolt pushes the spring back taut. When the trigger is pulled the spring is released, so that the bolt strikes the charge with force, which then explodes, sending the bullet down the barrel.

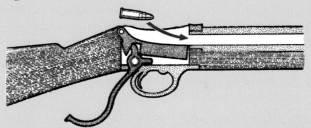

The Martini-Henry action

The lever was pushed down, opening the breech block. The cartridge was pushed into the chamber as the lever closed. Later the Henry rifle developed a magazine of sixteen cartridges, but was judged unreliable in action.

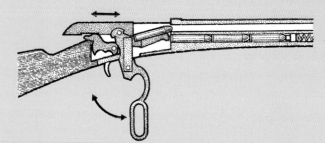

The Winchester repeater rifle

The Winchester was only issued in 1865. Cartridges in the magazine were fed into the chamber by moving the lever up and down, which moved the breech block back and forth, thus re-cocking the hammer.

patent). The base of the Minié bullet expanded after firing so that it gripped the rifling of the barrel; with such a gas-tight fit, the spin doubled its range and accuracy and reduced the number of misfires. The penetration of the Minié bullet was its most important quality. In the Crimean War it was reported that the Minié had 'been seen at 400 yards to go clean thro [sic] 3 or 4 Russians and kill them all'. Effective fighting ranges were increased to 300–600 yards and whole regiments of Russian infantry were seen to 'melt' before British infantry at the battle of Inkerman in 1855. Obviously, the main result of placing the Minié bullet in the firing line was that it increased the combat power of infantry *vis-à-vis* other arms. It was calculated that 150 soldiers armed with the Minié were equal to 525 with the musket.

The Prussian version, the Dreyse breech-loading rifle (or 'needle gun'), was operated by a bolt and fired a paper cartridge. It had an inferior range to the Minié but had a faster rate of fire – up to seven shots per minute compared with the Minié's two. Even more significantly, it could be fired lying down so that fire discipline did not depend on men standing in well-ordered ranks in the open. The Brown Bess muskets carried by Wellington's infantry in the Peninsular War (1808–14) would have been recognized by Marlborough's men a century earlier. The invention of the cylindro-conoidal bullet heralded an exponential increase in infantry firepower, even when muskets were adapted to take the new bullet.

Due to the enormous expense involved, there was no comparable advance in artillery technology before 1865. A breech-loading 6.5-inch rifled gun dated from 1845–6. During the siege of Sevastopol of 1854–5, the Allies brought up a battery of muzzle-loading, smooth-bore 68-pounders and 8-inch guns that had been converted to rifling. Additional rotation was achieved by the shape of the barrel rather than from grooves, as the shell moved around the barrel. These batteries were supplied by traction engines that hauled trains of wagons loaded with shells over difficult country from distant supply bases. In the field, Napoleon's technique of concentrating his guns into grand batteries

A Rodman Columbiad, c. 1863. This huge 15-inch calibre gun would normally be mounted on iron rollers to give the gun an all round traverse.

was imitated. Further, decisive results demanded the defeat of the enemy's guns, and this required counter-battery work: the suppression of fire so that the infantry and then the cavalry could move forward. But the greater range of the Minié bullet required that artillery action take place with much more circumspection. The gun line had to be kept to the rear or gunners became vulnerable to infantry fire and artillery pieces could be seized. The Duke of Wellington's record of having never lost a single gun during his campaigns would be much more difficult to emulate in the future.

The main tactical result of these improvements in weapons technology was an intense desire to increase the decisiveness of general actions fought commensurate with the level of weapons deployed. Here was a difficulty, however. Envelopment appeared to be the secret of victory bequeathed by Napoleon. Yet envelopment often permitted the enemy time to organize an orderly retreat because of the amount of ground that the attacking troops had to march over; gaps opened up between groups of tired men attempting to stay close to each other on the battlefield. The concentration of artillery firepower into grand batteries also prompted generals to consider the *penetration* of the enemy's centre. To shatter his cohesion here would result in a complete rout. The casualties tactical penetration risked were compensated for by a reduction in the difficulties of co-ordination. Traditionally, the arm that consummated the pursuit was the cavalry; but this was an expensive and fragile arm that offered a large target to the Minié rifle. Here was a conundrum that no nineteenth-century general solved successfully. Generals sought decisive, Napoleonic victories just at the time when this aim became more difficult to achieve tactically.

As far as strategic movement was concerned, there were two significant developments: the spread of the railway and the use of the telegraph. The railway had shown its military value as early as 1839 when the British government moved troops to deal with the Chartist demonstrations. In 1846 the Prussians moved a corps of 12,000 men with attendant horses and guns to Cracow. The success of this move led to a survey of the military potential of railways for the Prussian Army. In 1850 the Prussians learnt an important lesson. Technological change at the strategic level increases vulnerability as well as improving offensive potential. At Olmütz

A Prussian artillery park established at the Buttes Montmartre a month after the fall of Paris, photographed in February 1871. Before surrendering, Paris had been bombarded by the Prussians, heralding the enormous increase in the power and range of artillery by the end of the nineteenth century.

in 1850 the Austrians moved 70,000 men into Bohemia to intimidate Prussia and prevent it from dominating the German Confederation of the Rhine which had looked traditionally to Austrian leadership. Such a rapid concentration was achieved by the use of the railway and co-ordinated by the telegraph. Prussia, unable to match it at this date, succumbed to Austrian pressure. A number of Prussian reformers around the person of Helmuth von Moltke saw the need to make Prussia the premier military power within Germany. Aware that the Austrian province of Bohemia allowed the Habsburg monarchy to concentrate its forces within three days' march of Berlin, they emphasized the importance of the weight of the initial blow in any future war.

A further demonstration of the strategic importance of railways – and their limitations – was given during the Franco-Austrian War of 1859. The efficiency of the French railroad system enabled Napoleon III to concentrate 130,000 men (half his total strength) and 129,000 horses in difficult country. Despite grave logistical shortcomings, this rapid move gave the French Army the initiative in the great battles of Magenta and Solferino. But the advantages conferred by railways were negated once the battlefield was reached; trains enabled more men to be moved to the battlefield, but once they had arrived soldiers had to fight their way across it – and in this contest the skills of the fighting general were pre-eminent. The battles of 1859 were decided by a delicate balance of indecision. Both Napoleon III and the Austrian emperor Franz Joseph were hesitant commanders who lacked confidence. The campaign was decided negatively by the general who took the longest time to make up his mind. Napoleon III was saved from defeat at Solferino by two factors: Franz Joseph was even more sluggish than he was, and the excellent fighting qualities of his soldiers compensated for indecision and lack of operational and tactical grip. Other generals of this period who showed comparable deficiencies were not to be so fortunate.

Thus the main advantages of the railway were in deploying armies in the first phase of the campaign (especially in moving troops to the theatre of operations), and in supply. Yet the railway is vulnerable to attack. It is a delicate and fixed means of transport and once the enemy's country is traversed, it can be easily disabled. Likewise, the telegraph improved communications between the government in the capital and the commander-in-chief in the field, but not between the commander-in-chief and his subordinates. Mobilization was speeded up, staff work was facilitated over ever expanding distances. But the telegraph was too delicate an instrument to be carried into battle itself, although it could often be found just behind the front line. The lines could be easily cut, or the enemy confused by tapping into his line and sending false messages. Consequently, the telegraph had little operational and no tactical impact. In addition, like all new methods of communication, it increased work and added to the pressures weighing upon commanders. The telegraph also increased the amount of bureaucratic activity associated with warfare and the amount of paper produced by staff officers. In short, the railway and the telegraph required a thorough overhaul of military organization.

In the American Civil War the telegraph was a very important means of co-ordinating military operations over great distances. It is difficult to estimate the precise number of telegraph operators, perhaps 1,000 to 1,500. One in twelve of these became a casualty.

After 1815 large armies had come to stay. They also became more national. The British government's attempt to hire mercenaries to help fight the Crimean War, in the same way that Hessians had been used in the American Revolution seventy years before, was probably the last such effort. France and Spain abolished their Swiss regiments; only the Papacy retained them. The Prussian system of universal military service conscripted only Prussians. The French retained the Foreign Legion and raised regiments of colonial troops but they were not used against whites; the opposition to the use of black troops in 1863 in the United States is testimony to the strength of that prejudice, although military expediency overbore it. Armies were not only large, but standing. The Habsburg monarchy's army had a nominal peace strength of 400,000 men which consumed 20 per cent of the total budget. Defence expenditure in Prussia devoured 50 per cent of Berlin's revenues. This was an enormous outlay and Prussian reformers after 1815 were determined to ensure that the army gave value for money.

The reformers, who included Scharnhorst, Gneisenau and the theorist Carl von Clausewitz, were conscious of Prussia's military weakness, surrounded as it was by potential enemies in the centre of Europe. The naval powers, like Britain and the United States, had no similar incentive to follow the example set by Prussia. Forty thousand young Prussians were conscripted each year for a period of three years (in the cavalry and artillery they served for a longer term), giving a minimum strength of 120,000 men; they then passed into the reserves for a further two years, thus providing another 80,000 men; then all men spent a further seven years in the Landwehr – the real field army. In times of crisis reserves returned to their parent unit. Compared with the numbers raised, the expense was slight as it was unnecessary to pay high wages to conscripts. Furthermore, this system gave the maximum manpower at the beginning of any conflict. Thus, unlike Britain or the United States, whose land forces were small, Prussia could either attempt to deter a conflict or launch a pre-emptive strike with overwhelming strength.

Moltke and his collaborator, General Albrecht von Roon, began to modify this system in the 1850s. They devised a territorial system whereby each army corps could be brought up to war strength by men drawn from the same locale. They knew each other and their officers and NCOs. Moltke then turned his attention to the Landwehr which had degenerated in the same way as the American militia had in the 1830s. The Prussian population growth allowed the annual intake of conscripts to rise to 63,000, and they were kept in the ranks for five years. This gave the front-line army and reserves 504,000 men with only 252,000 in the Landwehr. A professional edge was thus given to the army with minimum extra expense and the emphasis was shifted from the militia. Moltke was also aware of the political implications of these reforms; there was always a danger that the Landwehr would harbour strong liberal loyalties and so weaken the army as a conservative pillar on which the Hohenzollern dynasty rested.

The increased size of armies required greater control and better organization. The growth in the number of corps and divisions (many

Prussian Army smiths at the garrison vehicle park at Nüblford in 1864 preparing for the advance on Denmark. They are repairing damaged wheels.

of which would be required to undertake independent missions) spelled out the need for an understanding of *auftragstaktik*. That is to say, the commander states the aim of the mission and the subordinate is left to fulfil it as he sees fit. Obviously, an army of 40,000 concentrated in one position is easier to command than a dispersed force of 240,000. Once again, the Prussians were in the vanguard of military reform even though the French Army remained bathed in golden Napoleonic nostalgia with a reputation as the greatest army in Europe. In terms of experience and fighting quality such a judgement was justified, but not in terms of organization. The regular United States Army, for instance, was closely modelled on the French. They both shared a similar mission as an imperial constabulary relying on long-service regulars. Napoleon III's army had fought well in North Africa and Mexico, and it was in these campaigns that his generals had won their laurels. Many American generals who conducted the Civil War, if they had any experience at all, had gained it chasing Comanches and Apaches, or in the Mexican War of 1846–8. Skills of a quite different order were required when fighting a great war of continental dimensions.

It was in nurturing such skills that Moltke applied his unrelenting industry in the 1850s, aided by the good fortune that the Prussian Army was not distracted by the needs of empire. Moltke developed a system of uniform education and training for all staff officers. It was based on a cogent structure of doctrinal understanding at what is now known as the operational level of war. That is to say, the Prussian general staff was mentally equipped and had the confidence to conduct large-scale operations involving the co-ordination of very large formations at the crucial intersection between strategy and tactics. The Prussian general staff were 'advisers *and* executants'. They knew their commanders' minds because they had all been educated in accordance with the same precepts; staff officers could take decisions confident that they were the legatees of trust. They were more than just clerks who wrote out orders (as they tended to be in Britain, France and the United States). They made plans, issued the orders and then oversaw their execution. Such tight co-ordination was crucial in the conduct of campaigns because of the increase in the numbers of roads available for military use during the nineteenth century and the extension of the frontage of each corps. During the first decade of the nineteenth century the latter had grown from 1.2 to 2.5 kilometres. It would continue to grow.

In the forty years since Waterloo a number of significant developments had altered the structure of war-making and led to certain changes in military organization. But military innovation never occurs in clear-cut sequences, and old and new methods commingle; the potential for change is often only glimpsed and its implications misunderstood. Generals had to accept rapid transformation of the weapons at their disposal; occasionally they employed a new weapon ineptly. The more intelligent of them understood that they were passing through a period of transition. General Sir John Fox Burgoyne, the British Inspector General of Fortifications, conceded that 'it is impossible to stand still and therefore the least imperfect [weapon] must be used until further improvement shall be devised'.

Emphasis on the influence of the Industrial Revolution can also mislead, important though it was. Britain, France and the United States, and especially central Europe, remained predominantly rural in the mid nineteenth century. Finally, the stress laid by historians on the evolving structure of western armies should not obscure the reality stated so tersely by Napoleon, namely, that in war it is the man who counts. In his book *The Historian's Craft* (1954), Marc Bloch contends that 'Behind the features of landscape, behind tools or machinery, behind what appear to be the most formalized written documents, and behind institutions, which seem almost entirely detached from their founders, there are men, and it is men that history seeks to grasp.' Behind telegraph offices and railway timetables, staff officers, gunners, engineers and all the logistical paraphernalia of armies, lay the commander. Pressures on him remained constant. To overcome them he required skill at judging what qualities were needed at each level of command, and, perhaps in equal measure, good fortune.

CHAPTER ONE

The Crimean War 1854–6

The raising of the tricolour symbolizes the fall of Sevastopol to the French Army in 1855. After 1815 the French Army's ethos came to resemble the British, mainly due to its experiences of colonial warfare, especially in North Africa. Also, since the conquest of Algiers, North African Zouave regiments had become fashionable, with short waistcoats, baggy trousers, cummerbunds and fez (or turban). Americans imitated the French style and several Zouave volunteer regiments were formed North and South before the Civil War. The painting certainly provides ample testimony of the reckless courage of the Zouaves.

The Crimean War

THE HISTORY OF WAR is replete with paradoxes and mysteries. One of the most curious is that during the nineteenth century the most industrially advanced countries were those initially least affected by the creeping industrialization of war. A combination of their geographical isolation and the maritime and industrial advantages that they enjoyed – as well as their constitutional sensibilities and hostility to standing armies – allowed Britain and the United States to maintain a minimum of military preparedness. It was the poorer and less advanced European economies, Austria, Prussia and Russia, that maintained the largest armies, with Prussia in the vanguard of organizational innovation. France, with a large army of long-service regulars, was somewhere in between.

The self-imposed isolation of the United States from the shifts in the European balance of power tended to conceal from Americans the great importance of allies in military calculations, and the role of outside powers in intervening, or failing to intervene, in shaping the wars of this period. The Crimean War is the only example of a coalition war discussed in this book. Ostensibly, Britain and France went to war (with Piedmont) to support Turkey in her struggle against the expansion of Russian power in the Balkans. War between Turkey and Russia had broken out in 1853. The Allies' pretext for intervening was a dispute between the Roman Catholic Church and the Greek Orthodox Church over the supervision of the revered Christian shrines in Jerusalem. The new, insecure (army-installed) regime of Napoleon III's second empire needed success in war to bolster its faltering legitimacy, and vigorously supported the claims of the Catholic Church. The Russian tsar, Nicholas I, rallied to sustain the position of the Greek Orthodox Church. Napoleon III hoped to use victory over Russia to underpin French hegemony in central Europe; this region was showing signs of consolidating into nation states in Germany and Italy that would be detrimental to French interests.

Great Britain needed success in war to tip the balance of power against Russia. Should Constantinople fall to the tsar, then the security of British naval lines of communication with her Indian Empire would be threatened. This was the 'Eastern Question' that used to vex the proverbial British schoolboy before he became preoccupied with gender studies. It was not love of the regime which prevailed at the Porte that prompted the intervention of the British, but cold, strategic calculation. Nevertheless, the extent of Russian ambitions was exaggerated by Britain. 'Mutual fear, not mutual aggression,' A. J. P. Taylor believed, 'caused the Crimean War.' Britain and Russia were the only two world powers and Britain was becoming distressed by the growth of Russian naval power in the Baltic and the Black Seas. Turkey was a valuable British trading partner in the Near East; her purchases of British goods rose from £1.1 million in 1825 to £8.5 million in 1852. But a great gap was to emerge that was never successfully filled, between Britain's diplomacy and war aims and her strategy.

The Crimean War involved a broad campaign against Russia along naval lines, including naval operations in the Baltic which are outside the scope of this book. The focus here will be on the military operations conducted in the Crimea itself; but the reader should be aware that this was only one theatre of operations. The Crimean War was a limited war for limited objectives; but such wars cannot be fought successfully with limited armed forces, and this was something that British statesmen found difficult to understand. Although the British government organized a 'war cabinet' to oversee its conduct, throughout the war Russia was allowed to raise great war loans on the London money market.

The British Army that was committed to the Crimea has a popular reputation for resembling a museum piece. It is often supposed that the shock that this obsolete force, commanded by genial old buffers, windbags and empty-headed aristocratic idlers, received during the winter of 1854–5 generated a programme of urgently needed military reform. In actual fact, the reform of the army had begun before it set out for the Crimea in September 1854. Since 1830 the reformers had introduced a programme of increased professionalization, as witnessed by the foundation of the Royal United Services Institution and the growth of a military literature that largely focused on tactics and technical matters. Formations and staff work had been rationalized, with a proper divisional and brigade structure. An attempt had been made to attune manpower to commitments and the administration of the army had been improved. These last two matters were complicated by the great importance of colonial soldiering for the British Army –

which had done much to nurture the regimental system – that made it difficult to concentrate on the preparations needed for a great European war.

The weaknesses of the reform programme were, however, revealed starkly by the actual conduct of operations in the Crimea. The force dispatched to the Crimea under the command of Lord Raglan was only 26,000 strong, and many were new recruits. There was no reserve because all other troops were deployed in the empire; here was a classic example of what is called today 'over-stretch': the soldiers sent on operations were over-worked, became over-tired and were

This superb photograph of Lord Raglan, taken by Roger Fenton, captures his gentility, serenity and also his aloofness. Although much maligned by the press during the winter of 1854–5, there was no one better to take his place.

thus vulnerable to infection. The Crimea, in any case, was a difficult area in which to operate, even for a small army. Its barren and bleak uplands rendered impossible the usual policy of requisitioning supplies. Raglan was keenly aware that the commissariat was wholly inadequate. Transport was decrepit, the men could not cook because of the lack of firewood and their resulting malnutrition left them weak in the face of disease. The problem was compounded by an inability to distribute the insufficient supply of medicines. The administration of the army was also split into too many competing departments, all with their own fastidious and elaborate bureaucratic procedures. Dynamic action under pressure was not their strong point.

Raglan would have had a difficult job on his hands even if he had been better served by his administrative structure. The commander-in-chief was under the misapprehension that he was conducting a defensive war on behalf of Turkey. He was not privy to the cabinet discussions on the aims of the war, and he showed little interest in the important naval objectives in the Baltic. After the Turkish naval defeat at Sinope on 30 November 1853 British public opinion demanded the seizure of Sevastopol. Raglan wrote that the choice of this objective was 'decided more in deference to the views of the British Government than to any information in the possession of the naval and military authorities, either as to the extent of the enemy's forces, or to their state of preparation'.

An air of illusion pervaded strategic discussion. The Prime Minister, Lord Aberdeen, abhorred war and was easily swayed. The First Lord of the Admiralty, Sir James Graham Bt, a powerful and persuasive advocate, believed that sea-power would be decisive, and that spirit and determination would compensate for inadequate ships. Graham argued that control of the Black Sea would check any Russian advance through the Balkans; a move on Sevastopol, moreover, would cut Russian sea lines of communication and allow the British to attack a variety of other objectives. Graham realized that the most enticing target was Russian naval power in the Baltic Sea. Once the Black Sea was neutralized Graham preferred to concentrate his naval resources on controlling the Baltic, and destroying the Russian naval bases at Sweaborg and most important of all, Cronstadt. To achieve this aim the Black Sea had to be neutralized, and this in turn required the destruction of Sevastopol and the Russian fleet.

These ambitious operations were essentially joint – because they demanded the intimate co-operation of the army and the Royal Navy – and combined because they rested ultimately on an alliance with France. Mutual suspicions characterized this alliance, as they tend to do. Tensions with France remained; there had been recent periodic invasion scares, and colonial rivalries festered. Old suspicions died hard; for nearly 200 years Britain and France had found themselves in different warring camps, and Britain had placed herself at the head of the alliance that had eventually overthrown Napoleon III's uncle. Raglan had been Wellington's military secretary at Waterloo and could not rid himself of the habit of supposing that the French were the enemy. At meetings of his staff he would cause the French liaison officer much uneasiness by declaring: 'At 11 a.m. tomorrow we will march on the French!'

The objectives set for Raglan's army, alas, were far too ambitious. The needs of the army and the Royal Navy were viewed in isolation and the problem was not considered strategically as a coherent joint operation. Sevastopol, by default, became one of the main objectives of a war being waged by a shaky coalition government. The majority of Raglan's subordinates were opposed to the plan to seize Sevastopol. General Shaw Kennedy believed that such a scheme was 'most absurd and dangerous'.

The consensus of military opinion was that the fleet and dockyard at Sevastopol could be destroyed only after a methodical campaign with a large army. This view contradicted the Admiralty's notion that a 'Grand Raid' like Copenhagen (1807) would lead to the early destruction of Sevastopol and to a rapid neutralization of the Black Sea. Raglan knew that he lacked any base save for the fleet. The use of steam-powered ships, crucial to sustaining the army advancing on Sevastopol, was therefore a hazardous gamble. The most sensible plan was gradually to occupy the southern part of the peninsular, then dominate its northern plains by cavalry action, and only then, once the Allied army was strong enough, commence the siege; but such methodical operations demanded an army of 100,000 men: in September the Allied force numbered only 53,000. It also required a measure of planning and preparation that the British military system could not provide – especially under the pressure of bringing a limited war to a rapid and successful conclusion. The Admiralty's confidence that the Black Sea could be neutralized swiftly was more palatable to the cabinet and the naval view prevailed. By comparison, the army's leaders were weak, fumbling and inarticulate. They failed signally to ensure that its doubts about the efficacy of the campaign were grasped by the cabinet.

Raglan's troops were landed on the beaches of the Crimea in the third week of September 1854, and on 19 September began their southward march to Sevastopol under the heat of a remorseless autumn sun. The French Army, commanded by Marshal St Arnaud, was on the right flank nearest to the coast, covered by the fleet. The British were on the more exposed left flank, drawn up in two columns of two infantry divisions each. The French had little cavalry, so the British cavalry division of a heavy and light brigade, with a total of 3,100 officers and men and 3,000 horses, was vital to the progress of the campaign – though inadequate for the strenuous demands that would be made on it. Initially, the Allies only had available the 600 men of the Light Brigade as the Heavy Brigade was not landed until after the battle of the Alma. Raglan and St Arnaud were commanding a large-scale raid and they needed to show above all that they could seize opportunities and act decisively. However, they lacked unity of command, were weak in intelligence and, even at this date, had no agreed strategic objective. The French kept changing their minds over the efficacy of besieging Sevastopol. The French siege train was left behind in Toulon, and, once the French were convinced that Sevastopol had to be taken, it took some weeks to catch up with the Allied armies.

As for the Russians, Fabian delaying tactics were forced upon them in the defence of their homeland. The Russian commander, Prince Menshikov, could be rash and careless in the heat of the moment. Yet he realized that his army was no match for the British and French in the field. His troops were still armed with the musket, were badly trained and showed a plodding disposition in battle, completely bereft of initiative or even good sense. Menshikov decided to hold Sevastopol and take up a defensive position along the River Alma. He was handicapped in building up his forces by the lack of a railway between the Crimea and Moscow or St Petersburg. However, he enjoyed two advantages denied the Allies. He possessed unity of command and the talents of Colonel Franz Totleben. Totleben was one of the great masters of siegecraft of the age. When Totleben arrived in Sevastopol he found its defences in a rudimentary state; he soon applied his formidable energies to correct this state of affairs. Despite his weaknesses in infantry and cavalry, Menshikov's artillery and engineers were initially a match for the Allies. Had the Russian Army even been remotely strong enough to launch an immediate counterstroke against an enemy force strung out over a barren upland, with long lines of communication, it could have been victorious. Raglan's doubts about the operation were more than justified. Yet he laboured conscientiously to make the best of things, hoping that Wellington's peerless example would see him through.

Raglan was, in many ways, an admirable man – courteous, considerate, a perfect exemplar of the gentlemanly code. He had served Wellington faithfully for many years and had observed his methods at close quarters. However, Raglan's entire military career had been served on the staff; he had never commanded a formation in battle. The Alma was to be Raglan's first battle. He imitated Wellington's aloofness, but was too kindly to be convincing. Besides which, he lacked Wellington's force of character, especially his driving energy and imperious manner.

At the Alma, Menshikov's position stretched for six miles, but his reconnaissance had been faulty because he failed to notice a small track that could carry guns, crossing his left flank. The French commenced the attack, in a battle where the tactics were no different from any fought in the Napoleonic Wars. In many ways the Alma resembles Borodino (1812) on a smaller scale. The French soon found the exposed track and began to move over it with naval gunfire in support. Menshikov panicked and began pulling troops from his right to cover it; fortunately, they played little part in the battle because by the time they had taken up position it was all over. St Arnaud, stricken with the cholera that was sweeping through the entire army, told his two senior subordinates, 'With men such as you I have no orders to give. I have but to point to the enemy.' This remark was all too accurate a description of the level of generalship displayed at the higher level. The French advance then ground to a halt. Canrobert, the senior corps commander, intimated that if the British did not attack, the French Army would pull back. Raglan, whose relations with St Arnaud were good, was alert to inter-alliance sensitivities and immediately launched a frontal assault, even though the British faced the most rugged sector of the Russian position.

Raglan, like St Arnaud, gave no orders himself. He simply stated that the British battle line, which stretched for two miles, was to move forward and not stop until the River Alma was crossed. This instruction was beguilingly simple, but overlooked the complication that the real strength of the Russian position lay beyond the river. Raglan then moved away from the centre, where his subordinates could easily consult him, and took up residence on an inaccessible outcrop almost within the Russian lines where he could watch the fighting. He behaved more like a curious spectator than a commanding general. His only contribution was to call up a battery of guns that proved critical during the British infantry assault. The Russians had built two commanding redoubts of breastworks. The great redoubt was placed in the centre behind which Menshikov massed twelve guns;

The Battle of the Alma. One British officer thought the defending Russians resembled 'the dense crowd you would see on a Derby day'. The attacking British infantry tended to bunch together, earning them the unjustified rebuke of Sir Colin Campbell, 'My God! These regiments are not moving like British soldiers!'

the lesser redoubt was placed to guard the Russian right on Kourgane Hill. The infantry were drawn up behind these formidable defences. The Russians had been trained to fight in columns and found the British method of fighting in long lines rather confusing. They stopped firing and orders were issued to limber up the artillery pieces. Equipped with the Minié rifle, the British troops swept forward, disposed of a feeble Russian counter-attack, and then seized the great redoubt. The Russian position had been pierced but not overthrown. On his own initiative, Sir Colin Campbell decided to attack the Russian right flank, taking the lesser redoubt by an audacious move that only suffered fifteen killed and eighty-three wounded. A great cheer erupted along the British line, and the battle was effectively ended in about forty minutes. British casualties were 362, the French about 500, and the Russians perhaps 5,500.

The victory was not followed up by a devastating pursuit. Raglan had only the Light Brigade with him and any error resulting in its loss would have been disastrous for the Allies. St Arnaud was dying from cholera, so any decisive *coup de main* launched against Sevastopol appeared out of the question, especially as the British siege train on its own was deemed inadequate to take the city. However, the Allied caution seems exaggerated when it is recalled that Menshikov withdrew northwards to maintain communications with the Russian hinterland, rather than pull back into the city. Raglan reluctantly compromised, moving south of Sevastopol to secure the ports of Balaclava and Kamiesch. The opportunity of taking the city while its defences were weak was passed by. The Russians moved north and the Allies moved south, both movements being undertaken with neither side having the slightest knowledge of the movements of the other. The capture of Balaclava did little to alleviate the British supply difficulties. It was found to have a port frontage of 75 feet. A nine-mile journey was then required before the front line was reached. The troops amused themselves plundering captured Russian baggage. One officer was shocked: 'French books and novels of an improper kind were not infrequently met with in the baggage of the Russian officers.'

The reason for the initial failures of the Crimean campaign lay not in the individual abilities of the British and French generals but in their failure to create a suitable command system. The mid nineteenth century was the heyday of loose command arrangements. Despite the worship of Napoleon, commanders adopted a style that encouraged seniors not to interfere in the activities of their juniors, so that tactical direction was often non-existent. Such an approach is excellent when command at all levels is imbued with similar doctrinal training; but it can be disastrous in the absence of training. The battle of the Alma was characterized by individual fragmented actions that lacked the guidance of a directing brain. The Allies won more by luck than by judgement. Likewise, tactics were not geared to an over-arching operational design. There was no agreed master plan; Raglan did not press for one, and in the event of disagreements with the French generals, tended to conceal his doubts, allowing the expediency of coalition politics to direct his course. The result was the kind of drift and piecemeal tactical action that characterized the battles fought south of Sevastopol in the months of October and November 1854.

Now that the opportunity to seize Sevastopol had been lost, Raglan favoured an immediate assault on the city, but the new French commander, General Canrobert, was reluctant to throw his troops against the Russian defences. A long period of inactivity ensued, as each side improved its works. The Allies could bring the guns of their fleet to bear, but Sevastopol's defences were powerful; one fort had almost 100 guns. During an artillery duel the Russians hit the main French magazine, which exploded, but the Allies struck back and British heavy guns blew away the Russian defences on their sector; as neither the British nor the French were ready for the assault, another opportunity slipped away. There were also logistical obstacles. Like all long-service troops, the British and French soldiers were soon happy to grumble. Customary attention to dress was neglected, buttons were undone and necks open. The soldiers of the Crimea began to look very like their counterparts in the American Civil War. Many had 'nothing perceptible but their noses which appear from a dense forest of beard and whiskers'.

On 25 October Menshikov decided to strike at the Allied lines of communication and moved on Balaclava with 25,000 men. The two brigades of British cavalry were deployed north of the port and Raglan ordered two infantry divisions to their support. But before they arrived the Russians had seized several redoubts along the Causeway Heights. Raglan was anxious that the cavalry did not engage until the infantry came up. Throughout, his strategy had been to conserve the cavalry for its crucial intelligence duties, and he did not wish its strength to be frittered away on fruitless assaults. However, a 'black looking mass' of

Russian cavalry moved on to the Causeway Heights and cut through the important Woronzoff Road which ran to Sevastopol.

The stage was now set for the battle of Balaclava, one of the most famous actions in British military history. The commander of the cavalry was the Earl of Lucan, a petty, querulous and ungenerous officer, noted for his caution, and not thanked for it by his command. The Heavy Brigade was commanded by Major General Sir James Scarlett, a brave and determined leader much liked by his men. The Light Brigade was commanded by the Earl of Cardigan. Cardigan was bloody-minded, selfish and thoughtless. He slept every night on his comfortable yacht, and was known scornfully as 'the noble yachtsman'. As the Russians crossed the Woronzoff Road, Lucan ordered the two cavalry brigades forward minus Cardigan, as he had yet to stir himself from his yacht. Cardigan's feud with his brother-in-law Lucan was famous. Cardigan was never a man to be magnanimous and always pursued a vendetta with relentless energy. His self-confidence and obsessiveness with the trivial were boundless. Lucan was probably jealous of the former and the latter provoked their endless bickering. The Marquis of Anglesey has described Cardigan, with every justification, as 'a cad of Olympian proportions'.

Raglan issued orders to Scarlett for the Heavy Brigade to charge and a large cavalry mêlée ensued which swept up some units of the Light Brigade. The Russians had failed to sharpen their swords (the British were not much better) and they were driven off by much larger men and horses in a valiant action. The Light Brigade was not sent in pursuit; if Lucan had shown more audacity then Balaclava might have been a signal victory. None the less, Raglan had gained the initiative and was keen to take back the redoubts on the Causeway Heights. The infantry still had not arrived from the heights, and, after his initial success, Raglan believed that it was safe enough to rely on the cavalry alone. In an effort to stir Lucan from his inertia, he issued an order stating that the cavalry were 'to advance and take advantage of any opportunity to recover the heights. They will be supported by infantry, which has been ordered to advance on two fronts.' Once again, Raglan was located on a high vantage point from which he could see the movements of the troops but could not be consulted. Lucan issued no orders of his own.

In some exasperation, Raglan sent Captain L. E. Nolan to give Lucan a further order to attack. Nolan was a typical example of the military renaissance that had occurred since 1830, and had published two books. This was not a recommendation in Lucan's eyes, for Nolan had a reputation for being conceited and opinionated. Lucan certainly resented his superior manner and was perplexed by the order. He could not make out the objective; he confused the redoubts with some other guns a mile and a quarter away behind which the 'dark looking mass' of Russian cavalry had retreated. Nolan did not help matters; with a melodramatic flourish he pointed down the valley: 'There, my lord, is your enemy, there are your guns.' Despite having received four orders, Lucan was still confused; indeed, Raglan was probably making excessive demands on his imagination and initiative. Raglan was certainly not an effective communicator, and he overlooked the fact that Lucan did not enjoy as good a view of the battlefield as he himself did. Under the strain Lucan seemed to lose his judgement. He lacked the ability to think logically under difficult and frustrating circumstances and he would then give way to bluster and unload the responsibility on to his subordinates. Nolan must have known that the true objective was to prevent the Russians removing the guns in the redoubts rather than those further up the valley, but he did not trouble himself to explain the matter to a general that he so despised. Cardigan questioned Lucan's order but expressed his willingness to carry out a charge down the valley.

The Light Brigade then charged, 'in capital style', in the words of Captain Morris of the 17th Lancers. Despite Nolan's frantic efforts before his death to change Cardigan's direction, the brigade rode into a three-cornered trap from which there was no escape. The Russian general Liprandi thought they were all drunk. Fortunately, Lucan had the sense to ensure that the Heavy Brigade did not also get swept into the ill-fated action. Cardigan lost 37 per cent of the 661 men who charged; this was not a great number in absolute terms but the Light Brigade as a cohesive force was destroyed. In terms of reconnaissance duties this was a disaster for Raglan. Lucan refused 'to bear one particle of the blame'. The whole episode indicated the calamity that can occur when a large measure of discretion is delegated to a subordinate who does not understand the intentions of his commander. The battle of Balaclava was not a defeat for the Allies. Menshikov's move had failed to dislocate the Allied lines of communication. That any members of the Light Brigade survived at all is testimony to the moral sway that the British enjoyed over the Russians.

The battle also reveals an underlying ambivalence about the use of cavalry. The line between heavy and light cavalry had become blurred because of the demands of colonial service. Cardigan's charge was essentially a heavy action. The aims of cavalry, said Lord Lucan, were 'vigilance and activity to ensure the safety of the Army from all surprise' and to 'procure all the information within their power'. It was not to attack the enemy 'needlessly'. Yet cavalrymen themselves refused

The Charge of the Light Brigade as popularly represented. After the action, Cardigan addressed the survivors, 'Men! It is a mad-brained trick, but it is no fault of mine.' Some responded, 'Never mind, my Lord! We are ready to go again.' Cardigan replied, 'No, no, men! You have done enough.'

'The Valley of Death' shortly after the Charge of the Light Brigade. The actual valley is narrower than contemporary artists' depictions of it. Even so, the Light Brigade occupied less than 20 per cent of its width. The charge itself, apart from thumping hooves and jangling bits, was carried out in silence.

to accept this role in its entirety, and Lucan was dismissed as 'Lord Look-on'. But when the cavalry departed from reconnaissance and screening – even when cavalry action was successful – its capacity to carry out its main mission was reduced. This contradiction underlay all cavalry activity before 1871. Henceforth, Raglan lacked a viable cavalry force, and in the winter of 1854–5 the Heavy Brigade was worn down carrying supplies.

After Balaclava Raglan wanted to continue to attack the redoubts, but Canrobert feared that such an effort would detract from his efforts to concentrate before Sevastopol and launch a decisive assault. Communications between the base and the growing siegeworks were laborious and exposed. It was also becoming clear to Raglan that the British Army would have to endure a winter campaign. Burgoyne claimed that what the Allies faced was not a fortified city 'but an *army* deeply entrenched in strong ground, and with an immense provision of heavy [naval] artillery'. Although the French were content to remain in their works before Sevastopol, Raglan concluded that he was too weak to besiege and protect his force simultaneously. He withdrew two infantry divisions and the Guards Brigade to shore up his right flank. These formations did not entrench, as Raglan believed that his precarious long line astride the Inkerman Ridge could be best defended by troops moving in the open as they had during the Peninsular War. Canrobert was very reluctant to provide Raglan with any reinforcements, as his force numbered only 40,000 to Raglan's 24,800.

Menshikov decided to launch a counter-offensive from Sevastopol with 120,000 men on 4 November. His plan was simple: to strike at Raglan's two divisions while they were separated from the French, and prevent an Allied concentration by means of two diversionary assaults on the French lines before Sevastopol. Menshikov's infantry were shrouded in the autumnal fog and took some British units by surprise, but these quickly rallied, and offers of help from Bosquet's division were refused. 'Our reserves,' replied Sir George Brown, 'are sufficient to take care of all eventualities.' Yet the Russian diversion against the French was successful because French infantrymen pursued them back to Sevastopol – to be repulsed with losses.

The ground over which the Russians attacked was very broken up with ravines and straggling brushwood that divided the Russian columns and confused their commanders. Raglan allowed his subordinates to command without interference as the fighting surged back and forth. To strengthen his line Raglan brought up two 18-pounders from the siegeworks, and the French moved up twelve of their heavy guns. The Russians were then driven back by a brilliant charge of the French Zouaves, the Algerians and the 77th Foot. At 1 p.m. that afternoon, under very heavy Allied shelling, Menshikov decided to withdraw back into Sevastopol. The Allies retained the Inkerman Ridge, but again there was no pursuit. Canrobert was insistent on this point, and after the earlier French repulse he was probably right. Allied tactics had been disjointed and fragmented. It had been a battle won on the British side

THE BATTLE OF INKERMAN

The battle resulted from a Russian attempt to break the siege of Sevastopol by striking at a fragment of the British Army while the French were distracted. The Russians attacked in overwhelming strength deployed in three columns; but this strength was not brought to bear decisively. The resulting encounter was chaotic. Major J. B. Patullo of the 30th Foot wrote that 'No orders were given from first to last but to advance.' Major-General J. L. Pennefather, commanding Second Division, held Home Ridge, but French reinforcements, especially on the left flank, were crucial in forcing the Russians to withdraw.

to Sevastopol **1**

Inkerman Ridge

Careenage Ravine

XX
JABOKRITSKY

4

88
Acton 49
RB

X
CODRINGTON

Karabel Ravine

Victoria Ridge

The Wellway

Home Ridge

RAGLAN

3GG

6

47

32 Light

49

CANROBERT

Chausseurs d'Afrique

Post Road

XX
2
PENNEFATHER

XX
BOSQUET

22 Light

Marine Inf.

Algerians

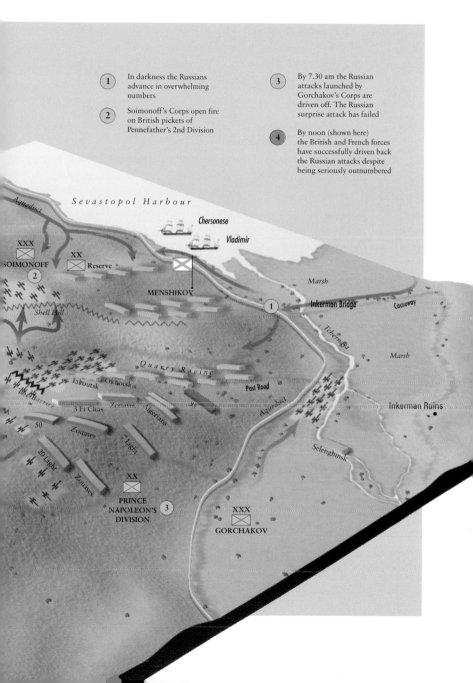

1. In darkness the Russians advance in overwhelming numbers

2. Soimonoff's Corps open fire on British pickets of Pennefather's 2nd Division

3. By 7.30 am the Russian attacks launched by Gorchakov's Corps are driven off. The Russian surprise attack has failed

4. By noon (shown here) the British and French forces have successfully driven back the Russian attacks despite being seriously outnumbered

Aqueduct

Sevastopol Harbour

Chersonese

Vladimir

XXX
SOIMONOFF
②

XX
Reserve

XX
MENSHIKOV

Marsh

①

Inkerman Bridge

Causeway

Shell Hill

Tchernaya

Marsh

Quarry Ravine

Iakoutsk   Okhotsk

Post Road

Inkerman Ruins

Harriet

3 Ft Chas   Zouaves   Algerians

50   Zouaves

Aqueduct

Selenghinsk

20 Light   Zouaves

Eagle

XX
PRINCE
NAPOLEON'S
DIVISION ③

XXX
GORCHAKOV

by the regimental officer. Sir John Fortescue was to write in his great *History of the British Army* that 'There was never a fight in which small parties of scores, tens and even individuals, showed greater audacity or achieved more surprising results.' It was the kind of fighting that the British excelled at, but they would be more firmly tested by the grim, exacting siegeworks around the Redan the following spring.

In the meantime British soldiers were forced to endure the hideous winter of 1854–5. Cold, wet and undernourished, the soldiers had to sit and freeze on the barren uplands around Sevastopol. In January 1855 the British Army in the field was 11,000 strong, with 23,000 sick or wounded. Visiting French officers claimed that French troops could never have endured such conditions so stoically. The men were dirty and unkempt. 'They look more like Cossacks' was the verdict of one visitor. The correspondent of *The Times*, William Howard Russell, who was to visit the United States in 1861 and provoke comparable outrage, telegraphed graphic reports to London that caused public anger and contributed to the fall of the Aberdeen ministry in January 1855. Lord Palmerston became prime minister, even though he was just as much to blame for the strategic mistakes as Aberdeen. Russell blamed Raglan and his staff – they were easy scapegoats. Improvements in communications demonstrated the new influence of newspapers on the conduct of war. Palmerston was willing to dismiss Raglan in a bid to demonstrate that he was doing something significant quickly. The Secretary of State for War, the Duke of Newcastle, replied that he was willing to dismiss anybody if there was any 'hope of saving the lives or health of the men'; showing a rare measure of nobility worthy of his distinguished title, he explained his unwillingness 'to recall men against whom there is a newspaper clamour and for whom I have no better substitutes; merely to save myself'.

Raglan worked himself to death attempting to alleviate the troops' difficulties. But he was too much a gentleman to be a truly effective leader. Detached and undemonstrative, he was the archetypical staff officer – unduly inclined to temporize rather than make a firm stand. On

Florence Nightingale at the hospital at Scutari, which she equipped as well as administered. 'Orderlies were wanting, utensils were wanting, even water was wanting,' she informed Sidney Herbert in December 1854.

many of the outstanding issues of the war, Raglan had been proved right; yet he lacked the strength of character to force his argument home.

The trench networks around Sevastopol presaged those that would strangle Vicksburg and Richmond in 1863 and 1864–5, and Paris in 1870–71. The same techniques, furthermore, would be required to break the deadlock. The British still held the left and the French the right flank. The Anglo-French front was too long for the troops available. It was dominated by two strong points, the Redan and the Malakoff; the French now held the Inkerman Heights. In March 1855 the Russians seized the Mamelon, halfway between the Malakoff and the first French trench. In response, on 9 April 1855, 520 Allied guns and 13-inch mortars bombarded the city, but Napoleon III was reluctant to allow an assault. On 4 May the Allies attempted to capture Kerch on the Crimea's eastern coast, in an attempt to strangle the city completely; unfortunately, the French withdrew their ships prematurely and the port had to be abandoned. Anglo-French relations plummeted; Sir George Brown claimed later that he wanted to hit Canrobert. The latter resigned and was replaced by General Jean-Jacques Pélissier, a fiery, ebullient, single-minded general in the best French tradition. At any rate, for all the changes in personnel (Newcastle was replaced by Lord Panmure), the Allies had made no progress since the battle of Inkerman, although the French Army was now 90,000 strong. On 26 May, at last, Kerch was taken, cutting the Russian lines of supply and rapidly destroying their cavalry.

The Allied command put its hopes in a massive assault to be launched on Sevastopol at 3 p.m. on 6 June. The huge number of wives, itinerant gentlemen and newspaper reporters all chattering about the forthcoming battle ensured that Menshikov would not be surprised by it. The French mustered four brigades for the assault, the British less than a battalion drawn from the Light and Second Divisions.

The French seized the Mamelon position easily and pushed on to the Malakoff where they were driven back; whereupon the Russians retook the Mamelon – although it was finally held by the French at the end of the day's fighting. It was while the attention of the Russians was fixed by the French attack that Raglan issued the order for the British assault on the Redan. It enjoyed the benefit of tactical surprise and drove the Russians right back to the core of their defences. The Redan was a truly formidable earthwork and taking it would highlight all the problems faced by entrenchments that would surface again during the American Civil War. The Redan was an earthwork about 70 yards long on each side with angles of 65 degrees. In front of it was a ditch 20 feet wide and 14 feet deep, from which the walls of the Redan then rose a further 15 feet. The total height of the escarpment was about 30 feet. In front of it were 450 yards of open ground. Running off from both sides were communication and support trenches. Until the Redan fell the British would have to devote much care, attention and organization to planning their attacks.

Such care was conspicuous by its absence in the attack on 6 June, for all the courage shown by the fighting troops. But subsequent trench warfare showed that courage alone would not take a powerful entrenched line. The staff work was puerile. Contradictory orders were issued; the reserves were too weak and far distant, and the intricate planning required was merely a glint in an ambitious staff officer's eye. The main fault of the operation was that the attacking force was simply too weak to carry out its grand objectives.

On 17 June the assault was renewed. Eight hundred Allied guns were to bombard the defences followed by an infantry assault at 6 a.m. Worried about the fate of the infantry crossing the fireswept zone in front of the Malakoff, Pélissier advanced the time of the assault to 3 a.m., and cancelled the bombardment, though he did not bother telling Raglan at first. When Raglan discovered the change of plan he agreed to it but kept in his own hands the time at which the British attacked. Obviously, the strength of the offensive would be greatly reduced if the assaults went in separately. In addition, the orders issued to the fighting formations were vague; little thought was given to the problems of attacking troops moving into parallel trenches, or how they should be deployed for the assault. The staff themselves lacked experience of trenches and were ignorant of the problems of moving 8,000 men forward under such conditions. Finally, each attacking brigade seemed to have its own idea of what it was going to achieve. In the absence of a single concept of operations, the battle threatened to break down, as every previous major engagement in the Crimea had done, into a series of piecemeal actions. Under trench conditions favouring the defender, this weakness would make undue demands on the morale and courage of the attacking units.

The synchronization of the offensive fragmented almost immediately. Russian musketry proved surprisingly effective, as the front rank received an already loaded musket from the ranks behind. The French infantry were halted in their tracks – not a single soldier was able to cross the ditch of the Malakoff. Any minor gains could not be consolidated because of the lack of reserves. Thus the British assault became by default the main effort, even though this part of the plan was supposed to have been a masking or diversionary move to cover the French onslaught. However, Raglan and his officers gained comfort from the knowledge that the attack was going forward on 18 June, the anniversary of the battle of Waterloo.

Due to a silly error, the covering fire provided by the artillery ceased prematurely. Accordingly, the Russian fire intensified. Raglan wrote afterwards that he had 'never before witnessed such a continuous and heavy fire'. The Russians had repaired their earthworks and behind the Redan's parapet were infantry, four ranks deep with muskets primed. The result was a foregone conclusion: 'fifty yards from the Redan', a witness reported, 'the fire was so heavy no mortals could stand it'. First of all the right wing and then the left collapsed, as British troops sought the shelter of their own trenches. At least Raglan had the consolation of seeing the centre hold steady. He ordered the artillery to open fire, which destroyed the Russian reserves massed in the trenches behind the Redan – even though artillery itself could provide no solution to the problem of how to get the infantry over it. The attack was then called off; ten days later Raglan himself died of cholera, weakened by overwork. He was replaced by Sir James Simpson. Simpson was an uninspiring grumbler, much preoccupied with logistics; he would have made a workmanlike chief of staff. He was certainly no improvement on Raglan, having already refused the command, rightly believing himself incapable of filling his lordship's place. He lacked ideas, had no plan and issued no orders. He seemed to be under the impression that the staff directed the army. He did not command.

During these anxious months, a visiting delegation of American Army officers watched the Allied preparations. Jefferson Davis, the Secretary of War in the Pierce Administration, had decided that there were many lessons to be learnt by studying the siege of Sevastopol. Much of the report that these officers wrote concerned technical matters, but the volume written by the most junior member of the team, Captain George B. McClellan, has more than a passing interest, as the author was to rise to be Union general-in-chief in 1861–2. Although McClellan's report emphasized the need for an offensive spirit to overcome fixed defences, there can be little doubt that witnessing the siege of Sevastopol had a profound influence on his military outlook. McClellan was much impressed by the steadfast Russian defence, and came away believing that all future war would be decided by intricate and deliberate set-piece action, often revolving around siegecraft. Further, although McClellan criticized the Allied generals for their failure to capitalize on their opportunities, his own generalship would demonstrate a caution and careful consideration verging on inertia.

The final onslaught on Sevastopol took place in September 1855. Simpson chose for the assault the Second and Light Divisions (those troops that had taken part in the attacks in June), rather than bring in fresh men. What passed for his plan involved a covering party of 200 men and a following ladder party of 320 to scale the Redan, whose gains would be consolidated by the storming party of a further 1,000 men. The Highlanders of Third Division were brought up as reserves, but no scheme was devised for them to be sent forward in an orderly manner. From 5–8 September 800 guns threw 13,000 shells and 90,000 round shot at Sevastopol's defences, with a further 250 French guns firing simultaneously, prefiguring the great artillery bombardments of the twentieth century.

The British aimed their attack at the salient of the Redan. This was a rather narrow objective, but considering the small size of the attacking force, it was probably justified. The great strength of the Redan was its open rear through which reinforcements could be poured. At midday the French infantry charged across the 250 yards that separated their trenches from the Malakoff. Pélissier had timed the successful French assault to occur in the middle of the Russian changing of the guard, and for a short period the works were unattended. Several other works fell, and unaccountably the Russians dispersed their overall effort in retaking these rather than concentrating on the Malakoff, allowing the French to slowly tighten their grip on it.

The British were not so fortunate. The Russians put up a stiff fight which soon wore away the strength of the small parties sent forward. The reserves were too far back – a tactical lesson that would have to be re-learned many times over the next seventy-five years. They had to traverse thousands of yards of trenches, which became congested; the men lost their way as well as their cohesion. At the Redan the nerves of the young soldiers, many of whom were raw and untrained, faltered, and they began to pull back. Just as they did so the escarpment of the Redan suddenly collapsed, burying many of them under quantities of earth. After two hours of fighting there were 2,447 British casualties, comparable to eight hours at Inkerman. The crucial turning point was the fall of the Malakoff. Prince Alexander Gorchakov, who had replaced Menshikov in February, decided that after this disaster Sevastopol could no longer be held. At 4 p.m. on 8 September he evacuated the city, withdrawing over a bridge of boats and screened by a raging fire. At last, after ten months, Sevastopol had fallen.

The main problem for the Allies was what to do with their victory. Pélissier and Simpson, after their exertions, were content to rest. Simpson, moreover, was more interested in making detailed preparations for another winter on Russian soil. Palmerston thought of widening the war further, and embarking on 'a real Baltic campaign'. The victories at Sweaborg and Kinburn in the summer of 1855 persuaded Palmerston that, with the co-operation of Sweden, Denmark and perhaps Prussia, a

The turning point of the Crimean War, the French seizure of the Malakoff. The attack was led by General (later Marshal) Macmahon. Every centimetre of the assault was contested bitterly by the Russians, so that each trench was fought over several times. The fighting lasted four hours and cost the French 7,500 casualties.

descent on Cronstadt was feasible. A victory here could open up the possibility of an assault on St Petersburg itself. The problem was that such amphibious operations in the Baltic offered little room for the deployment of a large field army in a region in which Napoleon III was uninterested. He certainly was not keen to undertake operations that would simply serve to augment British sea-power still further.

Napoleon III had always equated seizing Sevastopol with winning the war, and was keen to bring the Crimean adventure to an end. Austria issued an ultimatum indicating the grounds on which Russia should make peace; otherwise it might contemplate entering the war. Russia would then be completely isolated. Britain could not afford to act unilaterally because its field army was only 40,000 strong, while the French had 150,000 men. The Treaty of Paris, ending the war, was signed on 30 March 1856. The Black Sea was neutralized, thus presenting 'security against future aggression' and preventing the Russians from mounting an amphibious assault in the Dardanelles. The demilitarization of the Åland Islands secured Sweden's escape from Russian domination. In addition, the Declaration of Paris was signed outlawing privateering at sea and stipulating that 'Blockades, in order to be binding, must be effective, that is to say maintained by a force sufficient really to prevent access to the coast of the enemy.'

The first phase of the Crimean War, with its glittering uniforms and picturesque manoeuvres, gives the impression that it was an appendix to the Napoleonic Wars in which many of its commanders had served their apprenticeship. Yet such an impression is quite misleading. The Crimean War demonstrates the kind of influence that industrialization had on war in the mid nineteenth century. Technology and organization were crucial. Allied steam battleships had driven their Russian sailing equivalents from the seas and established complete supremacy in the Black Sea. This enabled the Allies to develop the lines of supply that were to sustain the Crimean expedition for over a year, despite great suffering in the winter of 1854–5. Such naval supremacy permitted the Allies to land an army 3,000 miles from home and then confront and defeat a more numerous enemy on its home soil. Allied weapons technology was also superior in every way. The Allies were equipped with the Minié rifle and (eventually) better artillery. Their superior manufacturing base produced ironclad warships, steam gunboats, long-range rockets and heavy siege guns, and their superior communications network enabled them to transport these to distant theatres of operations in a great arc of conflict stretching some 6,000 miles from the Black Sea to the Baltic.

Their lead in logistical and organizational terms allowed the British and French to fight a limited war while the Russians needed to mobilize an unlimited effort to resist them. Consequently, the Allies dictated the pace and conduct of the war; throughout they enjoyed the initiative, even when fighting in the enemy's country. Thanks to this asymmetry of effort, the British and French landed in the Crimea at the most opportune time. If Menshikov had been able to organize his defensive concentration sooner by the use of railways, then the uncontested landing made by the Allies would have been impossible. Nor is there any doubt that supplying the army would have been impossible using sailing ships. The Allies, and especially the British, suffered much in the winter of 1854–5, as the French were to do in the winter of 1855–6; but without steamships the siege of Sevastopol would have been untenable and an evacuation would have been forced, perhaps with catastrophic consequences. As so often in military history, however, the Allies had not planned a protracted attritional campaign before Sevastopol. Missed opportunities forced this upon them, and the techniques they were compelled to explore opened up new possibilities in the use of military power which many observers, like Captain McClellan, believed would open a new chapter in the history of war. Andrew Lambert calls the war of 1854–6 'the first modern conflict' because it was 'one in which technology and productive capacity played a major part'. Far from being a musty old museum piece fit only to be placed in the old curiosity shop of war, the Crimea is one of warfare's most crucial defining phases.

CHAPTER TWO

The Civil War: The War Takes Shape 1861–2

Major-General George B. McClellan stockpiled great quantities of artillery and cannon balls at Yorktown, Virginia in April and May 1862, in preparation for the final stage of his 'grand campaign' in the Peninsula that would end the Civil War with one blow. McClellan's vision resembled the Crimea. The war would be short but be concluded with a great siege – of Richmond – that would require immense stocks. Note the number of men absorbed by the logistical 'tail'.

The War Takes Shape, 1861–2

THE GREAT CIVIL WAR that engulfed the United States in 1861 resulted from a fundamental disagreement between its two most powerful sections, North and South, about the place of chattel slavery in the Union. Without the issue of slavery there would have been no war. It threw into doubt the very meaning of American freedom. To Southerners the greatest freedom they could enjoy was taking their property – their slaves – into every corner of the country, even where slavery had previously been outlawed. The Southern emphasis on 'states' rights' was essentially a coded phase for the defence of slavery – the South's 'peculiar institution'. The South did not go to war in defence of the right of its state governments to charter banks. During the 1840s a pro-slavery ideology grew up arguing that, by comparison with the brutality of industrial urban civilization, paternal rural slavery was a positive good. After the Compromise of 1850, slavery had made some advances and Southerners demanded not only that they should have the right to take their slaves into the huge domain of territory seized from Mexico after the war of 1846–8, but that Kansas should enter the Union as a slave state. The desultory violence that accompanied these demands provoked the growth of the anti-slavery Republican Party, which sought to restrict slavery to its existing limits. The depression of 1857, which hit the more industrial North harder, inspired the South with an exaggerated idea of the economic strength of 'King Cotton' grown by its system of slave-based plantations. When the Crimean War came to an end in 1857 the loss of new European markets for Northern cereals, previously supplied by Russia, added to the economic depression and darkened an atmosphere already marred by a sense of domestic crisis.

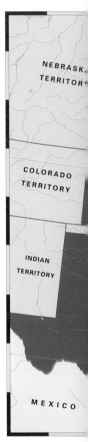

War itself was detonated by the refusal of the Southern states to accept as legitimate the election of the Republican candidate, Abraham Lincoln, in the presidential election of November 1860. Lincoln's

THE CIVIL WAR

In 1860 Abraham Lincoln carried all the Northern states except one. The South refused to accept the decision of the election, and thus raised the question, Lincoln claimed, 'whether a constitutional republic, or a democracy … can … maintain its territorial integrity'.

A Divided Nation
1861–5

Union states

allied to the Union

Confederate states

electoral victory was entirely sectional. He had won all the Northern states and 180 votes in the electoral college. Yet he had won only 39.8 per cent of the popular vote; in seven states he had not gained a single vote. In December 1860 South Carolina seceded from the Union. Georgia, Alabama, Louisiana, Mississipi, Texas and Florida quickly followed and proceeded to create their own Confederacy with its capital at Montgomery, Alabama. The new Confederacy desired to regain the sovereignty of all the federal military outposts within its borders, an issue that came to a head with the bombardment of Fort Sumter in Charleston harbour on 12–13 April 1861. Two days later President Lincoln issued a proclamation calling for 75,000 volunteers to suppress the rebellion. Curiously, the war came from a spark ignited by the side standing on the defensive. The federal government itself lacked the military strength to deter secession. The regular army consisted of

On 12 April 1861 the Civil War was provoked by the bombardment of Fort Sumter. A huge crowd had formed in Charleston harbour. 'The shells were bursting,' the diarist Mary Chesnut recorded. 'In the dark I heard a man say "waste of ammunition".'

about 16,000 men scattered over thousands of miles of Indian territory. Lincoln had to rely on the states to raise troops. Four slave states – Virginia, North Carolina, Tennessee and Arkansas – seceded rather than participate in the 'coercion' of their sister slave states, and joined the Confederacy. Their decision ensured that the two most important theatres of operations in the Civil War would be the South's most industrially advanced states of Virginia and Tennessee. In May the Confederate Congress took the decision to move its capital to Richmond, Virginia, thus giving Northern troops what appeared to be a more easily attainable objective, as it lay about 100 miles south of Washington DC.

On the outbreak of war strategic attitudes were essentially contradictory and tended to overlap and run into each other. Some Northerners believed that the task of physically occupying the South – an area about twice the size of the Union of South Africa – was beyond the strength of any army. They believed that the best way of ending the rebellion was by blockade (and Lincoln issued a decree announcing the blockade of Southern ports on 19 April) and other forms of economic pressure; once faced with the enormity of their actions, the Southern people would turn against secession; such a view was based on the assumption that persistent Southern Unionism would gain in strength and slowly but surely the seceded states would return to the Union. The leaders of this school of thought included the new Secretary of State, William H. Seward, and the general-in-chief, Winfield Scott. Scott was a 75-year-old Virginian of unimpeachable loyalty; but he was bloated with dropsy, and constantly grumbling about the state of his health. Despite his pessimism, the clarity of his intellect remained undimmed; moreover, he was the only soldier in America who had actually commanded an army victorious in battle, and his views therefore compelled respect.

The second view appears to be the exact opposite of the first, but is really an extension of it. If secession was an ideology of shallow roots and capricious loyalties, then it could easily be overthrown. Here was a society prone to see warfare in melodramatic Napoleonic terms, tinged with the rhetoric of the 'minutemen' of the American Revolution. Armies were thrown together in days, inspired by the nobility of the cause and its leaders, and victories won in decisive and sudden movements, without reference to the complications of weapons, engineers and logistics – let alone such arcane activities as planning. Men rushed to the conclusion that the war would be short and concluded by a single great battle. War was a simple phenomenon, its dimensions easily gauged by men of moderate ability. Command was not a difficult task; what was needed was drive, determination and an ability to lead; the growing political class of the United States produced such men by the thousand; the tiny size of the regular army was no handicap because of the bountiful talent of the 'genius' of the American people. At any rate, these two prevalent views implied little or no change in Southern race relations resulting from a quick Northern victory.

Notions of a short war were accentuated in the South by an unproven faith in the superiority of the 'Southron' as a fighting man. During his journeying in the South, William Howard Russell, the ubiquitous *Times* correspondent, was dismayed by the bizarre biological circumlocutions that Southern politicians deployed to justify their military superiority: Northerners were physically enfeebled by commercial activities; they sat in offices rather than rode horses outdoors; they were corrupt rather than vital, more interested in making money than in the manly activity of the duel. Southerners believed that they were the products of a military tradition. They were uniquely talented in the skill of arms. Had not the South produced both George Washington and Winfield Scott? In fact the Southern military tradition was a myth, one of many – like the curious notion that some Southerners (Virginians, in particular) were descended from cavaliers – that had been put about in an effort to emphasize the distinctness of the South. As many (if not more) Northerners as Southerners graduated from the United States Military Academy at

This photograph of Winfield Scott and his staff was taken in August 1861. He weighed 300 pounds (22½ stone) and could no longer ride without help. Even the junior officers were middle-aged. The officer on the far left is his military secretary, Schuyler Hamilton, grandson of Alexander Hamilton.

West Point but numbers of these then left the army for more lucrative jobs in business and industry. What is curious, however, is that many Northerners *shared* this Southern belief in their martial superiority. Northerners had grave doubts about the long-term effects of rapid industrialization and feared that it would corrupt their manhood. Such attitudes would lead many to doubt the nerve of Union commanders who had the ability to organize their men but not to lead them. Such fears would be ruthlessly exploited by Southern commanders in Virginia in 1862–3.

A residual belief in short wars was also related to the comforting reassurance of industrial strength. Here the capacity of the North was infinitely greater, although resources in themselves do not win wars. The total population of the United States in 1860 was 31,443,321. Of these the population of the Confederate states was 8,726,644, of which

3,953,760 were slaves. The Border states (including the District of Columbia) had a population of 3,588,729; if these fell to the Confederacy then overcoming secession would have become immensely difficult. Lincoln admitted that 'to lose Kentucky is to lose the whole game'. Yet to retain it ensured a Northern numerical superiority of 4:1, as the Northern population, including the western territories, stood at 22,716,657. Potentially, the North could thus mobilize 4 million fighting men to the South's 1,100,000.

Even with Virginia and Tennessee, the Confederacy had only one ninth of Northern industrial capacity. In 1860 the states of Massachusetts and Pennsylvania each produced manufactured goods that were worth twice the value of the entire South's production. Massachusetts alone produced more manufactured goods than the eleven states of the Confederacy. In 1860 the North produced 97 per cent of the firearms, 94 per cent of the cloth, 93 per cent of the pig-iron, and more than 90 per cent of America's footwear. The South could produce enough food to sustain itself but lacked the means to distribute it effectively. By 1860, of the 31,000 miles of rail track laid in the United States, only 9,000 miles could be found in the eleven states of the Confederacy. Indeed, the Northern track formed a cohesive network linking the 'Old North West' of Wisconsin, Michigan, Illinois and Ohio with the Atlantic seaboard. It was thus comparatively easy for the North to mobilize its resources and send them where they were needed. In the Southern states not only were there large gaps in the network but the track was laid on different gauges, making long journeys inconvenient and arduous. Of the 470 locomotives built before June 1860, only nineteen had been constructed by Southern engineers. Given this huge industrial disparity, Southerners placed great store by European intervention, provoked, they calculated, by a self-imposed embargo on 'King Cotton' that would starve European (especially British) textile industries of its regal threads.

When Lincoln had issued his proclamation in April 1861 calling for volunteers he had also called the Congress into special session. This was not due to meet until 4 July. Because secession had generated its momentum by exploiting the inactivity of the preceding Buchanan administration, Lincoln could not afford to wait. On his own responsibility he took the unprecedented step of organizing an army and paying for its armament without the sanction of Congress, justifying this strictly unconstitutional behaviour by virtue of his war powers; Congress was asked to legitimize his acts retrospectively. The 75,000 who volunteered to serve for three months were reinforced by a further 43,000 in forty regiments for three years. By 1 July 300,000 men had been raised, 208 regiments instead of forty. In the South the new Confederate president, Jefferson Davis, had been empowered to raise volunteers without reference to the state governments, and by August 1861 there were 200,000 men in the field.

The main problem facing both governments was equipping and housing these raucous but enthusiastic hosts. Even the palatial Congress was impressed as a barrack in an overcrowded Washington

A Confederate camp at Warrington Navy Yard, near Pensacola, Florida, in 1861. Note the studied informality, civilian clothes and bedraggled layout. Ignorance concerning camp organization and hygiene led to the spread of disease, which accounted for half of all casualties in the Civil War.

DC. In order to beat the Northern blockade the South dispatched purchasing agents overseas, but mainly to Britain, and bought 800,000 British Enfield rifles. The federal armouries at Springfield and Harper's Ferry soon embraced mass production, and by 1865 almost 1,500,000 Springfield rifled muskets had been manufactured, an achievement that remained unequalled in the nineteenth century. Only France came anywhere near challenging this level of production with the manufacture of a million chassepots in 1866–70. But the North, too, sent purchasing agents overseas, and by 1865 Union troops were using seventy-nine different types of personal small arms weapon.

The Springfield rifled musket was a muzzle-loader which weighed about 10 pounds, and fired a .58 calibre bullet to a range of 1,000 yards. The South manufactured its own version, and picked up large numbers abandoned by Northern soldiers during the string of Confederate victories in the summer of 1862. The South profited from the dynamism of several renegade Northerners, not least Josiah Gorgas, who virtually single-handedly created Confederate ordnance and built up the Tredegar Iron Works at Richmond and smaller installations at Atlanta. Although the breech-loading Spencer carbine and the Henry rifle were also issued, the Springfield was the basic weapon of Civil War soldiers on both sides. Even with the 'minnie' bullet, as the soldiers spelt the Minié, the effects on Civil War tactics of the Springfield were evolutionary rather than revolutionary. The effective range of the Springfield was around 250 yards – which was a 150 per cent improvement on the Brown Bess musket – with two to three shots fired per minute. But because the rifled musket was still loaded by ramming the bullet down the muzzle, an elaborate drill was required to organize firing, which still required men to stand in rows in the open. They would then fire their weapons in unison in volleys; but the range and speed of firing was, on average, five times greater than it had been in the Napoleonic Wars, with greater accuracy and with far fewer misfires. Consequently, throughout 1862, but especially after the autumn of that year, Civil War soldiers began to employ entrenchments. These would involve the digging of a shallow rifle pit perhaps 3–4 feet deep with a breastwork several feet high placed on top of this. In other words, Civil War soldiers built up – they did not dig down except in the formal sieges of fortified towns such as Vicksburg and Richmond. Breastworks were the only viable form of field fortification because of the continued need to fire standing up and in volleys. The 'repeaters', such as the Henry and the Spencer, were issued to the snipers and cavalry respectively; over 200,000 Spencer and Sharps carbines were made, but only 15,000 of the expensive and intricate Henry. So the Civil War was not, as it is sometimes portrayed, the war of the rifle.

None the less, the changes in tactics were the result of improvements in infantry weaponry rather than the artillery. That is to say, tactical development in the United States mirrored that in Europe. Although the machine gun first made its appearance in the American Civil War, it was the 12-pounder cannon, the 'Napoleon', that was the backbone of American artillery on both sides. This fired solid shot a distance of some 1,680 yards, and was not much of an advance on models used during the Napoleonic Wars; however, the ordnance was only about two thirds of the weight of that used over half a century previously and so could be delivered more quickly to the guns. The Napoleon also had the advantage of greater elevation and timed fuses which could explode the solid shot ball ten or fifteen yards above the heads of advancing infantry, thus maximizing the killing power. However, in the nineteenth century it was the weapons system rather than the munition which led to the increase in firepower; it was not until after 1870 that breech-loading artillery started to dominate battlefields, with improved explosives rather than the solid shot of muzzle-loading cannon, thus banishing breastworks from the scene. For the moment, Civil War artillery still had to be 'pointed' at the enemy by direct fire rather than calculating his advance behind obstacles and using indirect fire. Its most important role was in killing infantry in the attack, and not in supporting attacks by long artillery bombardments. Gettysburg would illustrate both of these roles. The Confederate bombardment on the third day was a waste of ammunition; the use of Union artillery to shatter 'Pickett's Charge' was devastating in its power largely due to grape or canister, which threw a cascade of lead balls or jagged metal pellets into the midst of infantry formations.

The Civil War was an infantrymen's war. The core of Union and Confederate armies consisted of their road-bound infantry. This was the most important arm, and victory could only be achieved by encircling enemy infantry or driving it from position. Mobility was therefore limited tactically and pursuit rare. The main difficulty in organizing an effective pursuit was not just the strength of infantry on the defensive, and can be explained by two other factors. First, insufficient attention was devoted to it during the planning stage. Second, the weakness of the effective mobile arm. American cavalry were dragoons, that is, mounted infantry, and were in no sense a *corps de chasse*. Given the increase in the range and effectiveness of firepower, and the size of the target offered by horsemen, that is just as well. However, the gradual removal of cavalry to the margins of the battlefield, or indeed to separate battlefields where entirely mounted battles were fought (unmounted, of course), meant that in the pursuit, men on foot chased other men on foot. They were not faster than the defeated – who were, after all, running for their lives – and this remained a tactical conundrum that was not seriously considered, let alone solved, by the end of the Civil War in 1865.

Once a sizeable army had been raised, pressure began to mount in the North for its immediate use. Hugh Brogan once observed of the American people that, despite their many attributes, they were not schooled for the long haul. The dazzling mirage of the Napoleonic victory beckoned. Winfield Scott believed that the volunteers needed to be trained. His critics replied that he was an old fusspot; the very point about the genius of the American people was that it was at its best unfettered. In correspondence with the newly recommissioned Major George B. McClellan, Scott advanced an idea that the decisive theatre of operations should lie in the Mississippi basin. Scott intended 'to envelop the insurgent states and bring them to terms with less bloodshed than by any other plan'. By taking advantage of the Union supremacy in naval power, Scott believed that twelve or twenty gunboats accompanied by forty river steamers could carry sufficient *matériel* for 80,000 men. The column would be divided into two: the smaller would operate on the river itself, the larger would move overland; together they would outflank and seize all Confederate strong points between the junction with the Ohio river and New Orleans. Scott's plan was strictly limited and attempted to insulate military operations from political and social pressures by shifting military operations away from the political heart of the rebellion in his native Virginia. However, politics kept breaking in, and Union strategy could not ignore the two most wealthy Confederate states, Virginia and Tennessee.

Scott feared 'the impatience of our patriotic and loyal Union friends', and this is what overwhelmed him when he presented his ideas to Lincoln's Cabinet in June 1861. The shift of the Confederate capital to Richmond had greatly agitated public opinion. Horace Greeley, the editor of the New York *Tribune*, who could not himself tell the difference between tactics and strategy, began a press 'clamour' with a headline 'On to Richmond'. The pressure was too great for the administration to resist, and Scott's grand design was shelved, although it was to be realized during 1862-3 by piecemeal approaches. However, the 'Anaconda Plan' (as it was designated by critical newspapers) shared a weakness that would be found in all strategy in the first year of the war. All assumed that one strategic thrust would bring about the collapse of the Confederacy.

This was an error committed by Lincoln's Cabinet on 29 June, when Brigadier General Irvin McDowell was ordered to take the troops gathered around Washington, now designated the Army of the Potomac, and seize Richmond before the Confederate Congress could assemble. McDowell was a conscientious and rather earnest officer, completely devoid of any sense of humour. Although he was more than conscious of the shortcomings of the troops at his disposal, he marched southwards towards the rail junction at Manassas. McDowell intended to hold the centre of any Confederate forces he encountered and then move around their left flank. His plan was respectable, even able, but it depended for its successful execution on Robert Patterson, a veteran of the War of 1812, who was to pin down the 10,000 Confederate troops of Joseph E. Johnston to their positions in the Shenandoah Valley. McDowell was harassed and overworked. When William Howard Russell arrived at Union Station in Washington DC he found McDowell looking for two batteries of artillery – hardly the job of the commanding general. He urged Russell to accompany his column. 'I have made arrangements for the correspondents of our papers to take the field under certain regulations,' he said solemnly, 'and I have suggested to them they should wear a white uniform, to indicate the purity of their character.' Not many generals since have

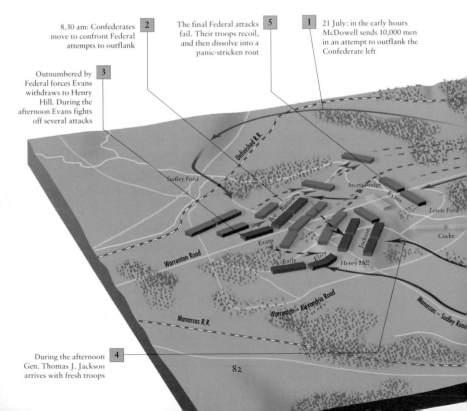

2 8.30 am: Confederates move to confront Federal attempts to outflank

5 The final Federal attacks fail. Their troops recoil, and then dissolve into a panic-stricken rout

1 21 July: in the early hours McDowell sends 10,000 men in an attempt to outflank the Confederate left

3 Outnumbered by Federal forces Evans withdraws to Henry Hill. During the afternoon Evans fights off several attacks

4 During the afternoon Gen. Thomas J. Jackson arrives with fresh troops shared McDowell's somewhat charitable estimate of the ethics of the fourth estate.

The great incapacity of General Patterson ensured that Johnston and his men slipped away southwards, boarding the train and permitting a Confederate concentration of some 25,000 men just north of Manassas Junction. The Confederate commander, P. G. T. Beauregard, a dapper Creole with an egotistic self-assurance bordering on conceit, was convinced that McDowell was going to turn his right and thus distributed his army perfectly to fulfil the goals of McDowell's

THE FIRST MANASSAS

The First Battle of Manassas (or Bull Run) 'epitomized', historian Marcus Cunliffe believes, 'the variegated confusions of a century and more of American warfare'. Its overwhelming civilian style, amateurish general and private soldier alike, and the pervading influence of 'politics' give it a symbolic as well as a strictly military meaning.

General P. G. T. Beauregard's vanity and superciliousness are well conveyed in this portrait. He was invariably appointed second-in-command or overshadowed by another. During his long periods of leisure he wrote to the newspapers, concocted absurd plans and intrigued against the Confederate president, Jefferson Davis.

plan. When the fighting opened on 21 July 1861 the First Battle of Manassas (or Bull Run) was to become the greatest battle fought in North America to that date. But the movement of formations was characterized by confused fumbling, with generals feeling more comfortable in the role of company commanders. For most of the morning the fighting had gone McDowell's way, but the *coup de grâce* was to be achieved by a long out-flanking movement which, in the event, would over-strain McDowell's troops. The crisis of the battle was reached shortly after 3 p.m. Under Johnston's coaching Beauregard had been switching troops from the right to the left, and they stood on Henry Hill as the Union column debouched on to the battlefield. In the scales of trepidation which weighed the faltering moves in this battle, the shift of small forces was decisive. The brigade of Colonel Oliver O. Howard was badly mauled and driven back from Henry Hill; the arrival of three regiments, two from South Carolina and the 28th Virginia, steadied the Confederate line, whereupon Union troops withdrew and then panicked. McDowell's retreat back to Washington was chaotic.

The first battle of Manassas ensured that the Confederacy would survive for a further year but did not guarantee its existence in the longer term. An increasingly fractious and bad-tempered dispute after the battle between President Davis and Beauregard over who was to blame for the Confederate failure to follow up the victory was really beside the point. The Confederates were lucky to win, were as disorganized by their success as the Union troops were demoralized by defeat, and nobody was prepared to exploit it. As for the North, this unexpected reversal would trigger off a round of soul-searching and strategic reappraisal. McDowell, although in his own eyes blameless (and he was not far wrong), was considered to have been besmirched by the set-back, and a new commander, who had won two minor victories in West Virginia, was called to Washington to take command. This was George B. McClellan. In a frantic search for a hero, and more in anticipation than in knowledge of his methods, the press instantly dubbed him 'The Young Napoleon', although McClellan was considerably older than Napoleon when he was first called to field command.

McClellan's period of command was one of consolidation, reorganization and rationalization; but it was also one of vexed controversy. McClellan was a brilliant trainer and the Army of the Potomac was created as a cohesive force, with strong morale, sound drill and sense of identity. McClellan began to promote his protégés to brigade and divisional command. The Army of the Potomac became McClellan's army, for he was adored by the troops and his influence persisted in the ranks long after he was there to nurture it. McClellan's skill as an organizer concealed a number of flaws in his character. In many ways he was an attractive figure. He had a sharp intellect, inspired loyalty and was master of his brief. On 1 November 1861 he was appointed general-in-chief to replace the ailing Scott. But time and experience – for McClellan's acquaintance with the battlefield was as yet slight – would reveal him as slow and indecisive; he was incapable of dynamic action even when all the cards were in his hands. He also refused to accept responsibility and tended to blame everybody except himself for his disappointments. He was too committed to the Democratic Party to inspire trust among his Republican political masters and, accordingly, he advocated the view that the war was for the restoration of the Union and not for any modification in the social system of the Southern states. A combination of his political faith and the enthusiasm with which he was greeted on his arrival in Washington nourished in his soul the delusion that he, and only he, could save the Union. Thus inspired he often acted in a conceited and high-handed manner.

By November 1861, despite his promotion, McClellan had already become the target of astringent criticism. His programme of training was not appreciated and the never-ending series of drills and reviews was ridiculed. This sense of disappointment was exploited by the Radical Republicans, many of whom believed that the Union's war aims should be broader than McClellan's emphasis on reconciliation, and should include the abolition of slavery. After a set-back in an autumnal skirmish at Ball's Bluff just outside Washington, on 20 December Congress created the Joint Committee on the Conduct of the War to oversee military operations. Not only did this body have the potential to compete with the executive branch in the organization of the armies, but it provided a forum for McClellan's critics to expound alternative strategies to those of the general-in-chief.

This groundswell of opinion reflected the obsession of politicians with happenings in and around Washington. In many other ways, the war was going well for the Union. By March 1862 it looked as if the optimistic view that the war would be short was the right one. The Confederacy suffered so many set-backs that it appeared unlikely to survive another summer. The blockade was tightening. A series of amphibious operations, including the capture of Hatteras Inlet and Roanoke Island in North Carolina in August 1861 and 8 February 1862, and the seizure of Port Royal on the South Carolina coast in November 1861, culminated in the fall of New Orleans on 24–5 April 1862. This last was a severe blow, as New Orleans was the South's greatest city and most thriving entrepôt. A Confederate victory in Missouri at Wilson's Creek in August 1861 was compensated for by the crushing defeat inflicted on Southern forces at Pea Ridge, which ensured the state's

Ulysses S. Grant's first major success – the seizure of Fort Donelson. Grant invested the fort and drove off an inept counter-attack. When the Confederates sued for terms, Grant replied: 'No terms except unconditional and immediate surrender can be accepted. I propose to move immediately upon your works.'

adherence to the Union and made advances into Arkansas possible. In the crucial Tennessee theatre, Ulysses S. Grant, with characteristic drive and energy, punctured the screen of defences laboriously patched together by the Confederate commander in the west, Albert Sidney Johnston, and on 6 and 16 February 1862 seized Forts Henry and Donelson. Grant's move exposed the city of Nashville, which Johnston evacuated on 25 February.

The deteriorating state of affairs in Tennessee demanded a counterstroke. Glad to have an excuse to be rid of him, Davis sent Beauregard to Tennessee as Johnston's second-in-command and effective chief of staff. Grant's troops had moved down the Tennessee river and disembarked from their river transports at Pittsburg Landing, near a small country church called Shiloh. Grant failed to entrench, despite orders to do so from his fastidious, clever but rather pedantic commander, Major-General Henry W. 'Old Brains' Halleck. Another Union column, the Army of the Ohio, commanded by Don Carlos Buell, a sour Kentucky slaveholder much preoccupied by indiscipline in the ranks and his logistical difficulties, was moving from the east

SHILOH

The battle of Shiloh, fought over two days, was a signal victory for Grant – although he could be criticized for being taken by surprise. The Confederates failed to exploit their initial advantage because they dispersed their fighting strength over too broad a front and lacked the reserve to follow-up successes. They attacked tactical objectives regardless of their value and neglected what was important – the need to cut Grant off from the Tennessee river rather than push him back towards it. Grant was given valuable time to consolidate his forces, and on the second day drove the drastically weakened Confederates from the field.

towards Grant. Johnston had concentrated 40,000 men near Corinth, Mississippi; Beauregard formed an operational plan closely resembling Napoleon's for the Waterloo campaign. He planned to strike at Grant's 42,000 men before they could unite with Buell's

1 6 April, dawn: Johnston's Army of Mississippi advances towards Pittsburg Landing intending to surprise and cut off Grant's Federal force

2 6 April: after initial skirmishing the Confederates drive forward but are held up on the Federal right

3 6 April, noon: throughout the day Federal forces hang on, giving ground very slowly, for seven crucial hours

4 6 April, dusk: Federal forces establish a solid position around Pittsburg Landing, driving back the last Confederate attacks of the day

5 6 April, 7 pm: a reserve division of Grant's army arrives and advances to join the Union right flank

6 6–7 April, night: General Buell's Federal Army of the Ohio reaches Pittsburg Landing, crosses the river and reinforces the Union left flank

7 7 April, 7 am–12 noon: General Grant now orders an aggressive counter-attack

8 7 April, 12 noon–2 pm: Confederate General Beauregard rallies his disorganized troops and mounts a tenacious defence

9 7 April, 4 pm: Confederate forces withdraw towards Corinth, leaving a victorious but exhausted Federal army in possession of the battlefield

TENNESSEE

to Crump's Landing

L. WALLACE

GRANT   BUELL
Pittsburg Landing   USS Tyler
USS Lexington

L. WALLACE (evening field)   McCOOK

XX SHERMAN   HURLBUT   CRITTENDEN   NELSON

Owl Creek

McCLERNAND

Water Oak Pond   Wicker Field
Bloody Pond
Hornet's Nest

BRAGG

POLK   Sarah Bell's Field

Shiloh Branch   Shiloh Church   Peach Orchard

BRECKINRIDGE   HARDEE

Tennessee

Eastern Corinth Road

to Hamburg

BEAUREGARD

to Corinth

20,000, Grant playing Wellington to Buell's Blücher. Johnston hoped to stack the odds in his favour by bringing the troops of Earl Van Dorn from the Trans-Mississippi, but Van Dorn lacked rail transport and only arrived after the battle.

Johnston's approach march in bad weather was chaotic and Beauregard advised withdrawal, convinced that surprise was lost. Johnston showed admirable determination in continuing the attack, and announced grandly: 'Tonight we will water our horses in the Tennessee river!' Like Waterloo itself, Shiloh was indeed a near run thing. On 6 April 1862 Johnston succeeded in taking Grant by surprise but dissipated his success by deploying his formations in a queue and then throwing them into the attack pell-mell without a reserve. As soon as the battle began, Johnston lost control and contented himself in directing small unit tactics. Exposing himself recklessly, he neglected a leg wound and died that afternoon. Grant, by contrast, kept his head and patched up his defensive line to gain time for Buell to come up. The fighting was ferocious in the thick rutted woods, especially around the 'hornet's nest' in the centre of the Union line, but its valiant defenders gained Grant the afternoon, and by evening Buell's men were being ferried over the Tennessee. The following morning Grant ordered a counter-attack and Beauregard, now in command, abandoned the field in confusion. Neither army was very large, even by Napoleonic standards, yet casualties constituted more than 25 per cent of the men engaged, 10,699 Confederate to 13,047 Union. Despite his tactical errors, Grant had won a signal, strategic triumph. Halleck came on the scene, took overall command of the two armies, and added a third, John Pope's, fresh from its success in seizing Island No. 10 on the Mississippi. With an army of 130,000 men Halleck crawled laboriously towards Memphis, which Beauregard abandoned on 6 June. The outer shell of the Confederacy had been fractured, and the important towns of Tennessee were safely in Union hands. Beyond, the Mississippi heartland now beckoned.

Jefferson Davis had decided to produce a defensive–offensive strategy based on the distribution of troops into departments. Forces would stand on the defensive to hold Confederate territory, then concentrate at threatened points and drive the Unionists back; troops would then disperse to hold the territory from whence they came.

Despite all his arduous labours and with chronic ill-health, Davis's strategy was gradually crumbling and it was difficult to see how the rot could be arrested, especially as morale sagged. In the North, all eyes were on McClellan to deliver the *coup de grâce*. Yet his 'grand campaign' to finish the war was a long time in coming. In December McClellan, weakened by the crippling burden of combining army command and the position of general-in-chief, succumbed to typhoid. The President, lacking any plan of campaign and made anxious by the rumours of McClellan's treachery, convened a council of war to advise him; McClellan rose from his sick bed to attend but refused to divulge his plans on the grounds of security. Throughout January the President issued a series of war orders in an effort to get the Army of the Potomac to move. In part, McClellan was a victim of a primitive command system which lacked a general staff to take much of the burden off his weary shoulders. He failed to focus on his prime duties as the government's principal strategic adviser and became immersed in the detail of army command. It was not until February 1862 that McClellan found the time to develop his ideas for the spring campaign.

McClellan's critics had only one essential idea: to repeat the campaign of the previous summer and march on Richmond via Manassas Junction. McClellan was convinced that he was outnumbered by the Confederates and believed that a repetition of First Manassas would lead only to bloody attritional battles that he would lose. He intended to avoid such deadlock by mounting an indirect approach towards Richmond via the Peninsula, between the James and York rivers. He would avoid the Confederate main strength, bring up his siege guns and batter Richmond into submission. In short, he would force the Confederates to fight for their communications and installations, and when they attacked, he would stand on the defensive in an 'American Waterloo'. McClellan's plan was an admirable essay in economy of effort, but it revealed his fundamentally defensive outlook, as well as the influence of his visit to the Crimea in 1855.

President Lincoln disliked the plan, partly because of the expense that a great amphibious operation would incur, but mainly because he feared for the security of Washington during the army's absence. But he sanctioned the plan so long as the city's defences were well provided for. Lincoln's fears were agitated first in March 1862 by the battle of the ironclads, the *Virginia* and the *Monitor* in Hampton Roads, which threatened McClellan's sea lines of communications; and second, in May, by 'Stonewall' Jackson's brilliant campaign in the Shenandoah Valley. McClellan moved his army by sea to the Peninsula and then inched his way up it, besieging Yorktown, which fell to his intricate and over-elaborate operations on 4 May. He took Williamsburg on 5 May and then based his lines of supply on West Point on the York river, which was connected directly with Richmond by rail. The Confederate commander, Joseph E. Johnston, was prickly, uncommunicative and cautious to his fingertips. He relied on Fabian delaying tactics, but rather resembled McClellan in his inability to reassure his political masters and produce an offensive plan. By the end of May, McClellan was only five miles away from Richmond but still waited for his siege guns to be hauled up. In the meantime, a Confederate concentration continued uninterrupted and Davis prevailed on Johnston to launch a counterstroke, which ended with the confused, poorly directed and indecisive battle at Seven Pines (Fair Oaks) on 31 May–1 June. Johnston was severely wounded and replaced by General Robert E. Lee, who had never before commanded troops in battle. His appointment was purely a temporary expedient until Johnston recovered.

Davis's action was his most important of the entire war. Lee and the Army of Northern Virginia, as it was now styled, became synonymous. Lee was the master of deception and calculated audacity. Manoeuvre and the lightning strike were the keynotes of his generalship. He also believed that Southern armies had to fight for the initiative, for only then could they avoid the weight of the enemy's overwhelming blows; if they remained passively defensive, they would be worn down and starved out in a siege. He thus presented Davis with an offensive design. He planned to shift the Confederate Army, almost 90,000 strong, north of Richmond and to bring crushing strength to bear on McClellan's exposed right flank. The Confederate cavalry, commanded by the flamboyant J. E. B. Stuart, had ridden round McClellan's entire army and confirmed that its flank was indeed 'in the air'. Lee planned to bring together on the field of battle the forces around Richmond and Stonewall Jackson's men, transported by rail from the Shenandoah. It was a brilliant plan, but it asked too much of tired and inexperienced commanders and raw and ill-disciplined troops.

Lee's counter-offensive did not at first go well. Jackson did not arrive on cue and A. P. Hill launched an unsupported attack at Mechanicsville on 26 June which was thrown back. Lee persisted and on the following day attacked at Gaines' Mill. This time Lee gained a tactical success; McClellan's reaction was to assume that he was about to be overwhelmed by masses of Confederate infantry and he ordered a withdrawal to the James river. Only one of his corps, Fitz-John Porter's V, had been involved in the fighting, and his plentiful reserves were still in hand, yet he abandoned his breastworks and offered Lee the supreme opportunity of enveloping his individual corps and annihilating

The man who saved the Confederacy in the summer of 1862 but prolonged the war – General Robert E. Lee. Handsome, courtly and charismatic. This photograph (taken in 1862) shows Lee at the height of his success. It also hints at his humility and shyness.

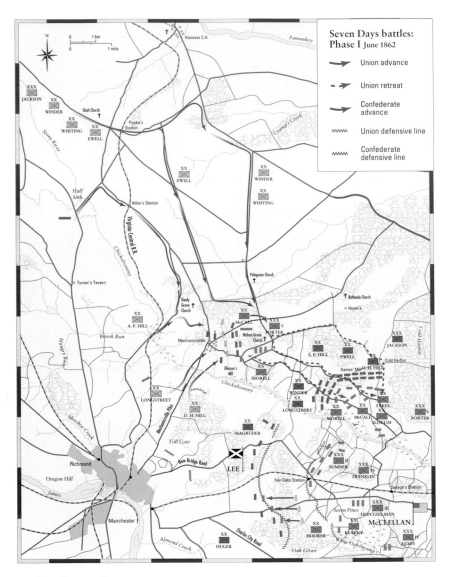

Seven Days battles:
Phase I June 1862

→ Union advance
-→ Union retreat
→ Confederate advance
〰〰 Union defensive line
〰〰 Confederate defensive line

THE SEVEN DAYS

The Seven Days battles form the Confederate counter-offensive before Richmond in 1862. As J. F. C. Fuller asserts, they show that actions, even 'though a tactical bungle', can have beneficial results. Thus, the Confederate success 'will always be considered as one of the great decisive strategical victories' of the Civil War. By a combination of

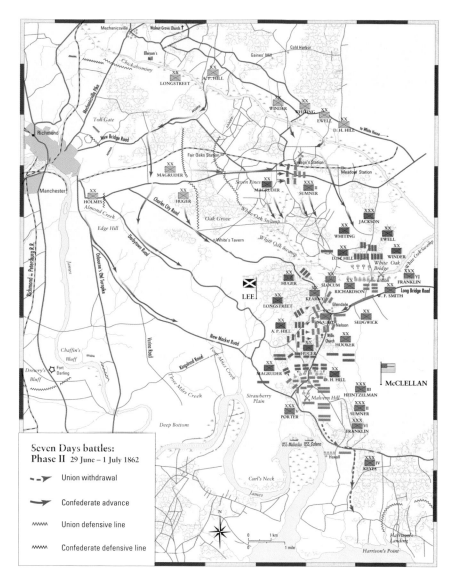

Seven Days battles:
Phase II 29 June – 1 July 1862

- - ▸ Union withdrawal

▸ Confederate advance

〰〰 Union defensive line

〰〰 Confederate defensive line

frontal assault (many repulsed) and envelopment that turned the Union right, Lee broke McClellan's overall cohesion. McClellan thought he was beaten, so he was. Confederate troops were thrown back at every turn, yet Lee knew that he could not only win, but destroy McClellan's army; he came very near to achieving his aim. His real victory was over the Union chain of command rather than over Northern troops.

them piecemeal. On two occasions, at Savage's Station and White Oak Swamp, Lee came close to achieving his aim, but Jackson was exhausted after his endeavours in the Shenandoah and failed to close the trap. McClellan withdrew to Harrison's Landing but before arriving there his artillery inflicted a harsh lesson on Lee's over-enthusiastic infantry at Malvern Hill. They attacked in surging broken lines, often without orders, and were driven back by canister. McClellen blamed the Lincoln administration for his frustrations, mainly because it had refused to release McDowell's I Corps which had been retained to protect Washington DC. Actually, McClellan had sufficient resources in hand to renew the campaign if only he had had the nerve to employ them effectively in offensive operations. Thus ended the Seven Days battles on 2 July. They were characterized by tactical errors and lost opportunities, yet they were an operational triumph for Lee because they gave him the initiative. McClellan did not stir himself from Harrison's Landing. The Seven Days were among the most decisive battles of the Civil War, for they ensured that the war would continue for some time. Robert E. Lee was determined, however, that it would end in 1862 with a Confederate victory.

The first stage of his new dynamic strategy was the reoccupation of the rest of Virginia and the consolidation of the northern frontier. Lee suffered 20,000 casualties in the Seven Days to the Union 16,000, but morale was high. He had concluded that speed of manoeuvre could compensate for the enemy's superiority of numbers and firepower, and he injected a much greater velocity into Confederate operations. Lee reorganized his army into two powerful corps, the first under James Longstreet and the second under Jackson. He moved northwards to confront a new Union Army, the Army of Virginia, being organized north of the Rappahannock. This was commanded by John Pope, who favoured more punitive methods against Southern civilians. Jackson moved around his flank, and as Pope withdrew, plunged into his rear, destroying his supply base at Manassas Junction. On 11 July Halleck was appointed general-in-chief (McClellan had been relieved of this responsibility before setting out for the Peninsula) and on 3 August, to

McClellan's fury, he ordered an evacuation of Harrison's Landing. Corps of the Army of the Potomac began to be withdrawn to reinforce Pope.

It became urgent for Lee to defeat Pope before the Northern Army became too strong and all the dividends of the Seven Days were lost. Jackson was 80 miles away, and Lee advanced to join him in a superb example of operational articulation on the old Manassas battlefield, via the Bull Run Mountains and Thoroughfare Gap. He linked up with Jackson on Pope's left flank in the midst of battle on 29 August. Pope was too preoccupied with attacking Jackson to heed warnings about the danger to his left. On 30 August Longstreet's Corps delivered a powerful stroke which shattered Pope's army and drove it back into the Washington defences. Only McClellan could rally this dispirited force and he was recalled to Washington once more to reorganize a reunited Army of the Potomac; Pope was dismissed.

Lee moved to consummate the initiative and crossed over the Potomac into Maryland. This was the second stage of his strategic design. By taking the offensive he could remove the burden of war from

Potomac Creek Bridge on the Aquia Creek Railroad. Built in 1862 by the US Railroad Construction Corps in nine days from standing timber. This feat reflects the investment placed in logistics by Union commanders.

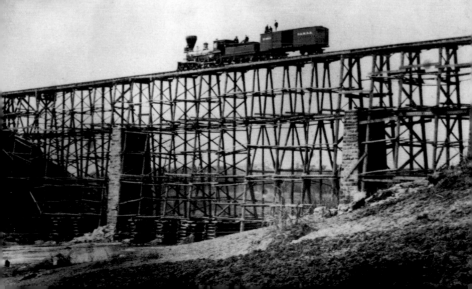

Virginia, subsist his army on Maryland's plenty, strengthen the Northern peace party in time for the November elections, and then win a victory on Northern soil and encourage Great Britain to intervene on the South's behalf. None the less, he believed that the South had to gain intervention by her own exertions, and not wait for outsiders to do her work while she sat idly by. The tone of Lee's correspondence gives the impression that he thought this was the climactic campaign of the war. He intended to stay on Northern soil for at least three months. Thanks to this upturn in the Confederacy's fortunes, Jefferson Davis attempted to organize a major Confederate counter-offensive along a front of 1,200 miles with his two major field armies. In Mississippi Beauregard was relieved of his command and replaced by Braxton Bragg, an effective organizer and disciplinarian, but morose, tactless and quarrelsome. Bragg immediately demonstrated his skill as an administrator, and his imagination and flair as a planner, by shifting his theatre of operations to East Tennessee. His army of 30,000 men journeyed to Chattanooga, Tennessee from Tupelo, Mississippi via Mobile and Atlanta, a trip of 776 miles over six different railroads. Bragg had exposed the flanks of the Union forces by his shrewd move and he at once commenced an invasion of Kentucky.

Yet the awkward command structure prevented Bragg from achieving a full operational concentration because he had moved out of his department, and the commander of the department into which he had moved, Edmund Kirby Smith, neglected to co-operate effectively, launching his own weak offensive further east. Bragg advanced on the state capital, Frankfort, intending to inaugurate a Confederate governor. Once he was installed, Bragg could legally conscript Kentucky citizens. These were markedly unenthusiastic about joining his army and reluctant to come forward to provide supplies. Bragg was forced to scatter his units to subsist. His opponent, Buell, had been careful to protect his lines of supply and fell back shielding his base at Louisville. After his concentration of 50,000 men was complete, Buell advanced towards Frankfort on a broad front. Bragg's senior corps commander,

Leonidas Polk, disobeyed Bragg's order to strike Buell's most easterly corps in the flank, with the result that Bragg had to abandon the inauguration ceremonies hurriedly and withdraw southwards towards Perryville. Intelligence on both sides was poor and the two armies collided in a meeting engagement near Perryville on 8 October. Bragg decided that the best means of defence was attack and launched a poorly co-ordinated outflanking thrust against Buell's left. The Unionists were driven back but Buell's two other corps had yet to enter the battle. By 8 p.m., when the fighting spluttered to an end, Bragg had won a tactical victory but, like Beauregard at Shiloh, could expect the full weight of Buell's counter-offensive the next morning. He withdrew from the battlefield, and then, on hearing of the defeat of his subordinates, Sterling Price and Van Dorn, at Iuka and Corinth on 19 September and 3–4 October, decided to abandon the campaign.

The eyes of the world were not on Kentucky but on Maryland, for here was what the great Prussian theorist Carl von Clausewitz called a 'centre of gravity' – the loss of which point would entail utter defeat for the Union cause. But by the time Bragg withdrew to Tennessee via the Cumberland Gap, Lee's campaign had already come to a premature end. He, too, had been forced to scatter his army to live off the country, and, by an act of criminal carelessness, one of the orders detailing this dispersal was lost and carried to General McClellan. He moved with unaccustomed celerity into south-western Maryland to cut Lee's army in two, but hardly with Napoleonic dash. He was held up in the passes of South Mountain and thus allowed Lee to pull the scattered fragments of his army together before Sharpsburg, south of Antietam Creek. But when the battle finally opened on 17 September, A. P. Hill's Light Division was still on the road from Harper's Ferry.

McClellan had managed to fritter away many of the aces at his disposal but he still held some good cards. Lee had only 40,000 men available while McClellan had almost twice as many. For reasons that are not clear Lee did not entrench, instead relying on the undulating ground for cover. However, McClellan threw away his chances of gaining a truly

PERRYVILLE

This was a lost opportunity for Federal arms. McCook's Corps, in search of water, was attacked by Bragg's army, but held its ground. Crittenden's Corps of 23,000 men was faced by only 1,200 Confederate cavalry. But Buell was not even aware that a battle had begun, and supposed that intelligence 'of serious import' would be sent to him. He should have gone forward, but he lacked operational grip, as his staff had decided to return to headquarters for their dinner; so Bragg could disengage and withdraw during the night.

(1) 10 Oct 1862, dawn: probing towards Doctor's Creek in search of water, Buell's left wing meets and engages Confederates. Sheridan's division drives them past Turbin house and digs in

(2) 10 am: Bragg arrives, orders Polk to attack Buell's left flank with Cheatham's and Buckner's Confederate divisions

(3) 2 pm: Confederates slam into McCook's Federal corps; McCook's front collapses. Across Doctor's Creek, Sheridan – under orders not to engage – watches disaster befall McCook

(4) Crittenden is unaware of the battle; bluffed by Wheeler's cavalry, his corps is not engaged

(5) 4.15 pm: Advancing along Springfield Pike, Powell's brigade attacks Sheridan but is repulsed. Sheridan pushes toward Perryville

(6) Late pm: Federals attack Confederate flank and chase Powell's men into Perryville. Finding themselves isolated, Federals withdraw

(7) Night: Buell brings up the rest of his forces to the battlefield. Outnumbered, Bragg retreats to Harrodsburg

decisive victory over Lee by his inept plan of attack. Instead of making the most of his great numerical superiority in a closely integrated, concentrated assault which would shatter Lee's thin line, he launched three separate attacks, first on Lee's left, then his centre; finally, Burnside's IX Corps attempted to cross the Antietam and take Lee's right in the flank, seize Sharpsburg and block Lee's retreat. The first two were thrown back by Lee's clever use of artillery in the defence and by musket volleys; but the Confederate infantry, standing out in the open corn fields or hiding in sunken lanes, paid a heavy price. Lee himself emulated Wellington at Waterloo and was ubiquitous on the battle-field, always available at the crucial point to take the important decisions; his behaviour contrasted with McClellan's torpor, distant at his headquarters in the rear, content to leave his corps commanders to fight their own battles without central direction, as he had done during

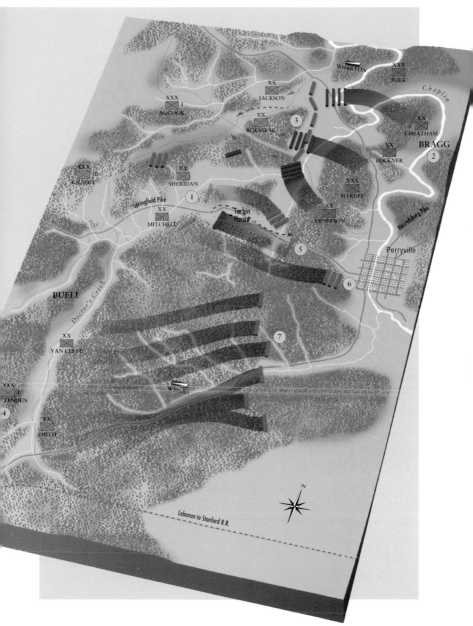

A Union signal tower on Elk Mountain overlooking the Antietam battlefield in September 1862. Signals were by flags (semaphore), experimented with by the US Army in the Indian Wars from about 1858. Flags were the preferred means of communication in the US Signal Corps from 1861–5.

the Seven Days. By his exertions Lee saved his army, although Burnside's thrust across the Antietam came perilously close to success, before being driven back in the nick of time by Hill's men coming up the road from Sharpsburg. Lee remained on the battlefield on the 18th, claiming the victory, which McClellan did not challenge.

The following day Lee slipped away to the Potomac fords, his great hopes for the campaign unrealized, largely due to a staff officer's slip – so often in war are great campaigns decided by the whims of the goddess of fortune. These hectic days in September had overstrained the stamina of Lee's men and the Army of Northern Virginia suffered much from straggling.

Lee's withdrawal offered great opportunities not to the South but to the North. Almost two months before, Lincoln had shown his cabinet a draft Emancipation Proclamation. The Secretary of State, William H. Seward, had cautioned him that McClellan's defeat was not an auspicious time to issue it, and Lincoln had put it aside. He now moved quickly to take advantage of the changed state of affairs, and on 22 September issued the Preliminary Emancipation Proclamation, which gave warning that all slaves currently held in Confederate territory would be freed on 1 January 1863. This was a major turning point, ensuring that the future history of the United States would take a completely new direction. In July, after his defeat in the Seven Days battles, McClellan wrote the Harrison Landing letter informing Lincoln that the war should be fought according to 'the highest principles of Christian civilization' – meaning that Southern lives and property (that is, their slaves) should be protected to ensure the continuity of the social system of the slave states. The Emancipation

Dead Confederate gunners from the batteries before Dunker Church. This photograph was taken by Alexander Gardner who, said the New York Times, *'has done something to bring home to us the terrible reality and earnestness of war'.*

ANTIETAM

Having lost his defensive line along South Mountain, Lee withdrew behind Antietam Creek, a tributary of the Potomac. It was six hours' march from Harper's Ferry, and Confederate units could either concentrate without fear of Union flank attacks, or withdraw back into Virginia. McClellan arrived on 16 September, but gave Lee a further day to consolidate his position. McClellan planned to strike Lee's left, and then his right. Then he intended to use the three centre corps, Franklin, Sumner and Porter, to shatter Lee's centre and destroy his army. But the plan broke down, because Lee discovered the move against his left and was prepared for it. As the battle developed, McClellan virtually abdicated command. He behaved like Tolstoy's Kutuzov in War and Peace, *convinced 'that the course of human events is predetermined from on high'.*

8 — 3 pm: Union forces launch assault toward Sharpsburg, pushing back Confederate units to the outskirts of the town

4 pm: Confederate reinforcements arrive from Harper's Ferry, a full division commanded by A. P. Hill. They advance immediately into the Union flank, forcing a withdrawal — 9

David Miller's cornfield

Nicodemus H

XX

L. R. JONES

JACKSON

STUART

Lee

WALKER

HOOD

Dunker Church

LAW

Barksdale

Cooke   G. T. Anderson   Kershaw

McLAWS

Ander

Colqui

LEE'S H Q

Sharpsburg

LONGSTREET

Bloody

Boonsboro Road

D. H. I

D. R. JONES

Evans

Toombs   Archer   Branch   Creek

XXX   IX

BURNSIDE

Brockenbrough

A. P. HILL

Burnside's Bridge

Harper's Ferry Road   to Harper's Ferry

Snavely's Ford

1 pm: Rodman's division crosses the Antietam Creek at Snavely's Ford and attacks Confederate units advancing on Union forces that are deploying after crossing by captured bridge — 7

10 am–1 pm: elements of Burnside's IX Corps capture a bridge across Antietam Creek after a bloody struggle — 6

Proclamation signalled that this would no longer prevail and, furthermore, that the North would embrace more revolutionary war aims than just the restoration of the Union. Lincoln intended nothing less than the destruction of the Southern social system. He was henceforth prepared to develop means of waging war that could fulfil the far-reaching goals that the federal government had now set itself.

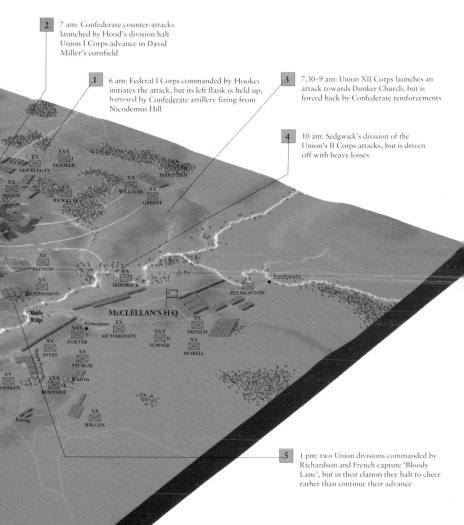

2 7 am: Confederate counter-attacks launched by Hood's division halt Union I Corps advance in David Miller's cornfield

1 6 am: Federal I Corps commanded by Hooker initiates the attack, but its left flank is held up, battered by Confederate artillery firing from Nicodemus Hill

3 7.30–9 am: Union XII Corps launches an attack towards Dunker Church, but is forced back by Confederate reinforcements

4 10 am: Sedgwick's division of the Union's II Corps attacks, but is driven off with heavy losses

5 1 pm: two Union divisions commanded by Richardson and French capture 'Bloody Lane', but in their elation they halt to cheer rather than continue their advance

CHAPTER THREE

The Civil War: The Year of Trial and Hope 1862–3

Union troops of Daniel E. Sickles' III Corps defend the Peach Orchard during the Battle of Gettysburg on the afternoon of 2 July 1863. The ground in Southern Pennsylvania was cultivated, and the undulating terrain offered open, broad fields of fire. Confederate movements could not be masked so effectively as they had in Virginia. The stone fences were valuable for building up improvised breastworks. We should be careful in assuming that all participants loathed their experience. Lieutenant William Wheeler of the 13th New York Battery thought 'the danger was so great and so constant that it took away the sense of danger'; he only felt 'joyous exaltation, a perfect indifference to circumstances'; he believed the three days of Gettysburg the most enjoyable of his life.

The Year of Trial and Hope, 1862–3

B Y NOVEMBER 1862 the Army of the Potomac still remained in the environs of the Antietam battlefield. McClellan did not follow up after Lee's withdrawal, let alone organize a pursuit. The President implored McClellan to move but he busied himself instead with logistical details. As Lincoln said, McClellan was a very fine engineer but he preferred a stationary engine. This was the worst case yet of a persistent ailment – McClellan's 'slows'. Lincoln finally lost patience and on 7 November, in a carefully timed move so that McClellan could not intervene in the elections of that month, he was ordered to hand over command of the Army of the Potomac to Ambrose E. Burnside. His emotional farewell to his troops symbolized the influence he had enjoyed during the army's creation. McClellan had promoted the great majority of the army's senior officers, and many shared his Democratic sympathies; but far more important for the conduct of the campaign in Virginia was McClellan's military legacy. He had impressed his fundamentally defensive outlook on his generals. Thus engineering and logistical priorities tended to receive more attention than operational manoeuvres, and the over caution which this attitude bred was easily transformed into an inferiority complex and lack of confidence. Drawing upon pre-war notions of a Southern military tradition, the Army of the Potomac tended to assume it would be defeated, and allowed itself to believe that Southern generals were better than its own. Lee's invincible reputation was worth a corps of troops to the Army of Northern Virginia.

But for all his exasperating faults, McClellan's departure left Lincoln with a knotty problem. The man had gone, but the system he had created remained. Lincoln had also taken the opportunity to remove Don Carlos Buell after the wasted opportunity at Perryville. Buell shared many of McClellan's worst faults without the saving grace of his charisma, and he was detested by his men. Both McClellan and Buell were utterly out of sympathy with Lincoln's policy of emancipation. Buell was replaced by William S. Rosecrans, an ambitious and quick-tempered Roman Catholic. Neither he nor Burnside had much experience of high command, and both were to be found wanting in this, the most exacting of all warfare's arts.

The North had shown that it could organize and equip large armies but Northern generals had yet to demonstrate that they had the skill, confidence and strength of character to carry forward offensive operations at the higher level; army command, where the final responsibility lies, requires different qualities from the command of a division or a corps. The Joint Committee on the Conduct of the War had a simple – and simplistic – solution to the command problem: Lincoln should dismiss all Democratic generals and appoint good Republicans, or at least those committed to emancipation. This would have caused

In October 1862 Lincoln visited McClellan, and urged him to advance after Antietam. Visiting the camps he asked a companion to name the force. He replied the Army of the Potomac. 'So it is called,' Lincoln replied sarcastically, 'but that is a mistake; it is only McClellan's bodyguard.'

more problems than it solved. Lincoln always gave great attention to mollifying loyal, Northern Democrats, and any purge on party political lines would have been deeply divisive. Besides, the Joint Committee's choice of generals was capricious and unreliable. But the seismic shift in the political landscape recorded after the issue of the Emancipation Proclamation had an effect, too, on military politics. Several of those who had served under McClellan, including Burnside and his senior corps commander, Joseph Hooker, began to express loud radical Republican sympathies. They immediately received the approbation of the Joint Committee's chairman, the uncompromising and uncouth Senator Benjamin F. Wade of Ohio. Burnside, previously an intimate of McClellan, was henceforth treated by loyal followers as an apostate.

Burnside had many fine qualities; he was genial, modest and brave. But he lacked confidence in himself, and his subordinates believed he was justified in taking this view. His first reaction on taking command was to disguise his weaknesses as a planner by taking refuge in a reorganization of the Army of the Potomac. He believed, probably rightly, that the army had too many small corps, and these were consolidated into three 'grand divisions'. He then shifted the line of operations eastwards to Fredericksburg on the Rappahannock river. He intended to exploit Lee's dispersal of his army for winter subsistence by crossing the river and driving on Richmond before Lee could concentrate to stop him.

The initial phase of the campaign went well. Longstreet was still in the Shenandoah Valley when Burnside arrived before the small, picturesque town of Fredericksburg. However, the advance ground to a halt due to a small error that had great consequences. The pontoons, essential for the crossing of the Rappahannock, were right at the back of his column which stretched some 25 miles to the rear. The delay in bringing them up allowed Lee to deploy Longstreet's troops, and he sent sharpshooters into the town to harass Burnside's preparations. Lee's position south of the Rappahannock was strong but not impregnable, and it made offensive operations difficult to develop because of the high ground on the north bank where Burnside deployed his powerful artillery. Lee would have preferred to withdraw southwards to the North Anna where he had found a perfect defensive position which promised decisive results. For this reason he did not entrench; but the opportunity that Burnside offered him, after his crossing of the Rappahannock was completed on 12 December, could not be passed up. The morning of 13 December was crisp and clear and began with an impressive parade of Burnside's army of 120,000 men. Lee's men remained behind cover until Burnside launched his attack.

The Union crossing had taken place at two points, one before the town itself, and another south and east of it, in a thickly wooded area. Burnside's greatest weakness as a commander was that he was a poor communicator; and he did not employ staff officers in whom he had confidence to explain the ideas which he expressed so incoherently. In truth, Burnside was incapable of imposing any order and structure on his plan. He launched a large frontal assault on Lee's centre. Lee's infantry were aligned in four ranks in a sunken road behind a stone wall which was better sited for defence than a similar position at Antietam. Behind them on Marye's Heights was the Confederate artillery. The combination of firepower was devastating. Longstreet's artillery commander, E. P. Alexander, predicted that 'a chicken could not live on that field when we open on it', and he did not exaggerate. When the central thrust was thrown back, Burnside decided to throw in his right wing, Hooker's grand division. In all, six great assaults were made on Longstreet's front (individual units made many more) but were swept back by rifled musket fire. No Union soldier got closer to Longstreet's position than a depression in the ground 100 yards away.

Burnside complained later that these assaults were supposed to be fixing operations, while a second outflanking attack, commanded by William B. Franklin with a reinforced grand division, cut Lee's communications, attacked his left and rolled his position up from the south. If this was true, then Burnside signally failed to make his design clear in the muddle that ensued, nor did he make much effort to impose

FREDERICKSBURG, 13 DECEMBER 1862

This battle seems an easy victory for Lee, but he could have been more severely pressed if the envelopment of his right had been properly co-ordinated with the attack on the centre. In the event, the former was held and the latter thrown back with ease.

V I R G I N

BURNSIDE'S HQ

Richmond, Fredericksburg & Potomac R.R.

Pleasonton

XX
HOOKER

XX
SYKES

XX
SUMNER

3

XX
GRIFFIN

XX
STONEMAN

BURNSIDE

Falmouth

GETTY

Rappahannock

1

Fredericksburg

2

Hancock

Howard

10

French

XX
BURNS

Marye's Heights

XX
FEATHERSTON

Stone wall

Washington

Sunken road

Washington artillery

Wilcox (Isla)

Wilcox (clts)

Wright

Perry

Ransom

Mahone

XX
Semmes
McLAWS

XX
R. H. ANDERSON

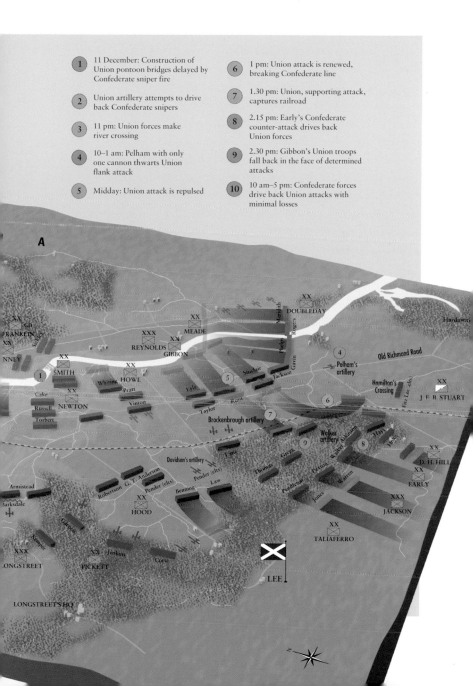

1. 11 December: Construction of Union pontoon bridges delayed by Confederate sniper fire

2. Union artillery attempts to drive back Confederate snipers

3. 11 pm: Union forces make river crossing

4. 10–1 am: Pelham with only one cannon thwarts Union flank attack

5. Midday: Union attack is repulsed

6. 1 pm: Union attack is renewed, breaking Confederate line

7. 1.30 pm: Union, supporting attack, captures railroad

8. 2.15 pm: Early's Confederate counter-attack drives back Union forces

9. 2.30 pm: Gibbon's Union troops fall back in the face of determined attacks

10. 10 am–5 pm: Confederate forces drive back Union attacks with minimal losses

A

DOUBLEDAY

Hardaway

FRANKLIN

Meredith

Rogers

Phelps

MEADE

NNLEY

REYNOLDS
GIBBON

Garin

Old Richmond Road

Pelham's artillery

SMITH

Sinclair

Jackson

Hamilton's Crossing

Fitz Lee (cav)

J E B STUART

Whiting
HOWE

Cake

Pratt

Lisle

Taylor

Brockenbrough artillery

Root

Walker artillery

Abraham

Hays

Russell
NEWTON

Vinton

Davidson's artillery

Lane

Thomas

Gregg

Pendleton
Paxton

Walker

Warren

Jones

Hoke

D. H. HILL

Torbert

EARLY

Armistead

Robertson

G. T. Anderson

Pender (cts)

Benning

Law

Pender (cts)

Jones

JACKSON

Barksdale

HOOD

TALIAFERRO

Garnett

Kemper

Jenkins

Corse

LONGSTREET

PICKETT

LEE

LONGSTREET'S HQ

his will on the battlefield. Franklin was a protégé of McClellan and fully lived up to the laggard standards set by that general. Three of his divisions, one commanded by George G. Meade, actually took Stonewall Jackson's troops by surprise and broke into their lines. Franklin was under the impression that his mission was to secure a bridgehead, and he was not a man to take a risk or seize an unexpected opportunity. The gift-horse rode away, its mouth firmly closed. Jackson organized a counter-attack with Hood's division loaned by Longstreet. It was Hood's furious attack that prompted Lee's famous observation, 'It is well that war is so terrible – we should grow too fond of it.' Here was a general who, unlike his Federal counterparts, actually relished the moral and intellectual challenges posed by fighting battles.

The completeness of Lee's victory and its one-sided character – Union losses were 12,600 to the Confederates' 5,300, including a lot of lightly wounded – provoked an immediate visit by members of the Joint Committee on the Conduct of the War. No doubt this was met by groans from the formation commanders, as they bustled about, declaiming on military matters of which they had a very slight acquaintance; there was hardly a military problem that could not be solved within ten minutes of their allotting it serious attention. The Joint Committee rallied to Burnside's support and Franklin was singled out as the culprit. Lincoln agreed, and he was relieved. Burnside obstinately continued to pursue operations on the Rappahannock but they ran into the mire in every sense. Senior officers made public statements about their lack of confidence in Burnside, and the roads were turned to liquid mud by heavy rains. Burnside was forced to return to Fredericksburg and was then relieved of his command on 25 January 1863 when he tried to remove his critics. The President was not without his critics either. The battle of Fredericksburg provoked a cabinet crisis, which he managed to overcome by adroit political tactics. If only his generals could have shown a measure of comparable skill! Union generals could organize and plan but they lacked the nerve to conduct great battles, and each successive defeat made the task harder.

General Joseph E. Johnston looking uncharacteristically decisive. He was very sensitive about precedence and rank, and distressed that he had not been appointed the Confederacy's senior full general. He thus spent too much time writing disputatious letters to Jefferson Davis. He eventually aligned himself with the President's political enemies.

Lincoln looked for relief to the west, but here the record was mixed. Grant moved on Vicksburg by the overland route across Mississippi. In December Van Dorn and a host of Confederate cavalry descended on his supply base at Holly Springs and utterly destroyed it. Grant was forced to withdraw and began to contemplate the immense difficulties of approaching Vicksburg downriver. Rosecrans made his base at Nashville and had decided upon a winter assault on Braxton Bragg's positions round Murfreesboro, the latter having returned to West Tennessee from his Kentucky perambulations. In an attempt to give Confederate operations some semblance of unity and stamp out the quarrelling among senior commanders, President Davis had decided to give Joseph E. Johnston command of the Department of the West. Johnston had now recovered from his wounds but was presented with a sticky problem. Mid-nineteenth-century America did not acknowledge the importance of theatre command; the essential role of generals was to command armies. Here the model of Napoleon did not offer much assistance because he had combined in his imperial person general-in-chief and head of state, and such autocracy went against the American republican grain. Johnston (like McClellan in the Union Army) did not know what was expected of him; as he did not command an army simultaneously (as McClellan had) he felt that he could not interfere with his subordinates who commanded in the field. He envied their position and gave them scant direction.

In December 1862 Davis conferred with Johnston and Bragg at Murfreesboro. Matters needing urgent discussion included which theatre of operations should have priority, Mississippi or Tennessee? Davis, unlike Johnston, always appreciated the importance of Vicksburg, overrode arguments for a maximum concentration in Tennessee, and sent Kirby Smith's corps of 12,000 men to Mississippi. This reduced Bragg's effective strength to 35,000. He was thus forced to await Rosecrans's move from Nashville, but he was not inactive. John Hunt Morgan was sent off on his 'Christmas Raid' through western Tennessee and did much damage to Rosecrans's supply lines. Nathan Bedford Forrest, a virtually illiterate former slave overseer of great toughness, also wreaked havoc west of Nashville. On hearing of Rosecrans's advance, Bragg moved forward to take control of the road junctions west of Murfreesboro. The fields were open and the woods could conceal an attack, but Bragg did not entrench. Rosecrans had actually caught Bragg napping with his army spread over a 35-mile front, but had been held up by the difficulties he faced co-ordinating his advance when relying on semaphore in thickly wooded country.

Both generals planned to attack; by a curious coincidence they adopted similar plans. Both intended to hold with their right and attack by enveloping the enemy's left flank. As they closed, the only question was, who would strike first? Bragg was more audacious than Rosecrans and launched his assault on the Union camps at 6 a.m. on 31 December. Surprise was complete, but as at Shiloh the woods broke up Confederate cohesion, and the Union troops were pushed back rather than shattered. Moreover, limestone outcrops made it all but impossible to bring up the Confederate artillery. Throwing canister in among Bragg's attacking infantry, Sheridan's division gave Rosecrans badly needed time to reorganize his line and prevent the Confederates from seizing the road to Nashville. Rosecrans was always at his best in defence, and his position astride Stones river was strengthened by refusing his flanks and placing a powerful grand battery of fifty-eight guns in his centre in an area called the Round Forest. The thick woods provided plentiful trees to strengthen his position with breastworks. He could thus sit it out and hope that Bragg would continue to attack him frontally.

Bragg was an imaginative strategist but a crude tactician. On 1 January 1863 after severe fighting Bragg had taken much of the Round Forest, but Rosecrans's army remained unbroken. On 2 January Bragg renewed the attack, this time switching the blow to the right and using John C. Breckinridge's division made up mostly of Kentucky troops. Breckinridge tried to cross Stones river but was confronted by Rosecrans's grand battery which had been pulled back to cover the fords. Bragg's acting chief of staff, Colonel Brent, wrote in his diary that 'A murderous fire was opened upon them … It was a terrible affair, although short.' Breckinridge's attack was the last in a long line of piecemeal assaults which threw away Bragg's chances of victory at Murfreesboro.

The increased strength of the defensive required a streamlining of tactical, offensive measures, but this did not happen. The American military system was incapable of such a far-reaching transformation, in any case, partly because of its amateurishness, but mainly because of the pressures resulting from hurried improvisation and dramatic expansion. Northern equipment and logistics benefited from an improvement in organizational techniques but not in the system for conducting operations. Consequently, both Union and Confederate commanders repeatedly failed to achieve tactical concentration supported by a close co-operation of arms. Great opportunities were thus wasted because they did manage to achieve effective strategic concentrations. On so many fields, not least Murfreesboro, attacks failed, even when complete surprise had been attained, because of poor technique in the attack, not because of any impregnability of the defence. There was a personal dimension to the problem. The favoured command technique in the nineteenth century was to delegate to subordinates. This had much to commend it, but it was used too frequently in the American Civil War by men like McClellan and Bragg, both of whom suffered from grave, neurotic weaknesses, to abdicate their responsibility for direction on the battlefield. Under such conditions it is not surprising that many infantry assaults were badly conducted.

MURFREESBORO DEC 1862 – JAN 1863

Bragg failed to defeat Rosecrans because of tactical error. Clumsy frontal attacks were repulsed. The artillery could not be deployed, and Rosecrans's line maintained its cohesion. His force was pushed back into a strong defensive position in a meander of Stone's river, while Bragg grew weaker and unable to deliver a final, crippling blow.

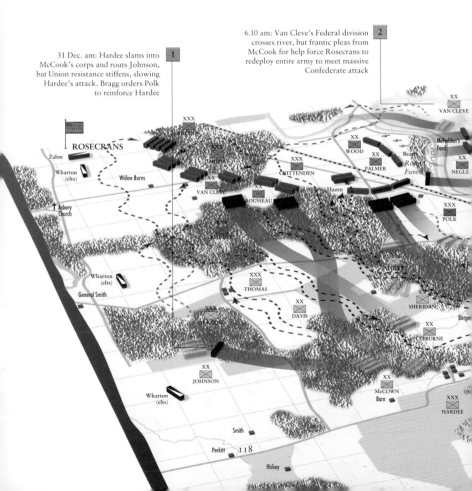

6.10 am: Van Cleve's Federal division crosses river, but frantic pleas from McCook for help force Rosecrans to redeploy entire army to meet massive Confederate attack **2**

31 Dec. am: Hardee slams into McCook's corps and routs Johnson, but Union resistance stiffens, slowing Hardee's attack. Bragg orders Polk to reinforce Hardee **1**

Lincoln greeted Murfreesboro as a great victory, which it was not. Affairs in Virginia were still grave. Lincoln needed a forceful personality to revive the fortunes of the Army of the Potomac. He thought he had found such a man in Joseph Hooker. Hooker had intrigued against Burnside, whom he despised, for months. Brash and boastful, a showman and a heavy drinker, Hooker replaced Burnside in the affections of the Joint Committee, because he had excoriated McClellan's memory and warmly supported emancipation. He set to his task with zeal. He abolished the grand divisions, improved the identity of individual corps

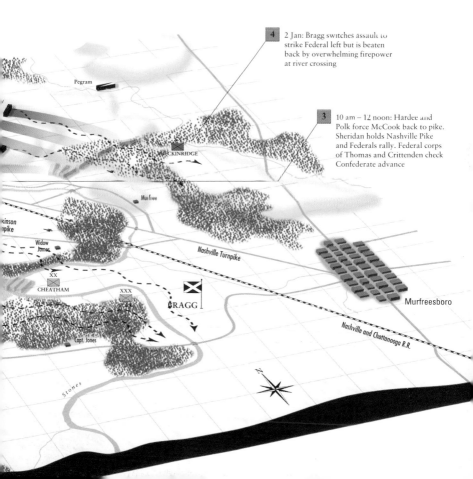

4 2 Jan: Bragg switches assault to strike Federal left but is beaten back by overwhelming firepower at river crossing

3 10 am – 12 noon: Hardee and Polk force McCook back to pike. Sheridan holds Nashville Pike and Federals rally. Federal corps of Thomas and Crittenden check Confederate advance

Pegram

BRECKINRIDGE

Murfree

Atkinson Turnpike

Widow Jones

XX

CHEATHAM

XXX

BRAGG

Capt. Jones

Nashville Turnpike

Murfreesboro

Nashville and Chattanooga R.R.

Stones

N

by giving each its own badge, centralized the command of the cavalry and managed to find the six months of back pay that the troops were owed; his popularity among the rank and file soared.

He had also drawn up an impressive plan for Lee's defeat – one of the most impressive of the entire war. He intended to move rapidly westwards, side-stepping Lee's strong position at Fredericksburg, then to cross the fords of the Rapidan and Rappahannock rivers, move through a tangled area of thick woodland known as the Wilderness and envelop Lee's left. Meanwhile, his cavalry corps, commanded by George Stoneman, would drive into the Confederate rear and paralyse Lee's lines of communication with Richmond. Dazed and disorientated, the Army of Northern Virginia would then be brought to battle under conditions that favoured Hooker. 'God have mercy on General Lee, for I shall have none,' he declared bombastically for the benefit of the newspapers and his radical backers. Yet it is indicative of McClellan's enduring legacy that Hooker's idea of a perfect battle was one in which he moved on to the defensive once he had cleared the Wilderness.

There is nothing wrong in principle with a plan that follows an offensive strategy with defensive tactics. It does assume, however, that the commander has sufficient flexibility to judge when the switch to the defensive is appropriate, and the nerve to see the campaign through to a successful conclusion. In the event, Hooker demonstrated that he lacked both these qualities. He was so proud of his plan that he treated it like polished marble: too perfect to be altered. And for all his bombast, Hooker, when in the top command, showed all the indecision of McClellan.

Not the least of Hooker's achievements before the campaign opened was his success in keeping any hint of his plan out of the newspapers, and Lee was baffled. Hooker was across the fords and into the Wilderness before Lee could move any of his troops westwards. The Army of the Potomac was 130,000 strong; never again would it be as numerous as when it advanced against its old adversary. Lee had

Joseph Hooker was one of the more colourful of the Army of the Potomac's commanders. In April 1863 President Lincoln visited the army. His arrival caused 'quite a commotion', with Hooker 'hustling off some of his female acquaintances in a most undignified way'.

62,000 troops, for he was without Longstreet who was subsisting at Suffolk. What Hooker's plan did not take into account was Lee's reaction. It did not occur to Hooker that Lee would match one enveloping move with another.

On 29 April Lee moved west with the bulk of his army. His men first made contact with Hooker's troops at a crossroads in the middle of the Wilderness near a house in the hamlet of Chancellorsville. Hooker at once called off the offensive movement and ordered his troops to dig in. This was a mistake: Hooker surrendered the initiative, and the congested vegetation provided a thick screen to cover Lee's movements. Hooker then paid the price for sending Stoneman off on his cavalry raid. Hooker lacked cavalry to screen his movements and provide valuable intelligence in this impenetrable country. Stuart quickly discovered that Hooker's unsuspecting right flank was exposed. Lee took the decision to attack it, and Stonewall Jackson was dispatched on the long approach march across Hooker's front. The Army of Northern Virginia was divided into small fragments, but they were attacked only by desultory movements as Lee moved ruthlessly to exploit Hooker's timidity. At 4 p.m on 2 May Jackson attacked Hooker's right and caused utter pandemonium, but he was mortally wounded before he could exploit his success fully.

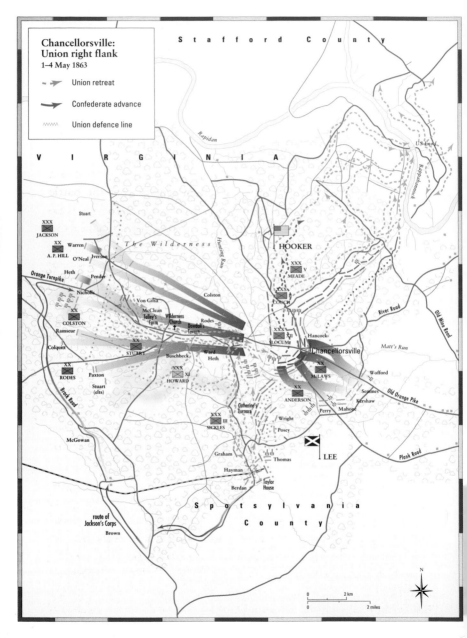

**Chancellorsville:
Union right flank**
1–4 May 1863

- ➤ Union retreat
- ➤ Confederate advance
- ⌇⌇⌇ Union defence line

Hooker himself was concussed when Confederate artillery opened fire on the Chancellor house. He ordered a withdrawal back to a fortified line between the Rapidan and Rappahannock rivers, thus permitting Lee's army to reunite at 10 p.m. on 3 May. Hooker still hoped to stick to his plan of getting into Lee's rear by ordering troops under John J. Sedgwick to cross the Rappahannock at Fredericksburg; but Sedgwick's timorous movements were too slow to achieve decisive results and he slunk off to seek shelter in Hooker's fortified camp.

Lee's victory at Chancellorsville was his greatest achievement as a field commander. But commentators often remark that the battle lacked strategic consequences. This is certainly true, but there is no mystery about it. Without Longstreet's corps, Lee could not hope to do anything more than drive Hooker back. His victory does underscore the importance of the personal factor. Lee's army at Chancellorsville was the same size as Bragg's at Murfreesboro but, for all his gentlemanly demeanour, Lee was the dominating intelligence, whereas Bragg, despite his hot temper, floundered in hesitation. As for Hooker, he fundamentally mismanaged his superior resources. He experimented with employing the telegraph to control his huge command, using his chief of staff, Daniel Butterfield, as a clearing house. Yet this innovation broke down, the technology failed to work, the operators were inadequately trained and Butterfield became swamped. The communications failure only served to accentuate Hooker's own weaknesses. In truth, despite his ability, Hooker was best suited to the corps level of command.

CHANCELLORSVILLE

This map concerns itself with the famous operations on Hooker's right flank, culminating in Jackson's flank march and envelopment of XI Corps. A Union envelopment of Lee's right was part of Hooker's plan but never proved dangerous. On 3 May, Lee divided his army again to deal with this at Salem Church to the east of Chancellorsville.

The laying of telegraph wire had become by 1863 a highly organized and intricate operation, often taking place just behind the firing line. The wire was sometimes strung in the trees initially and then transferred and fixed to the poles once they were erected.

Chancellorsville conferred on Lee one precious commodity – the initiative. Lee hastened to organize a second invasion of the North. Having lost the strategic initiative the previous autumn he intended to regain it by using operational initiative. Although the position was not so propitious, he calculated that speed and drive could restore the possibility of European intervention – especially if he could win a further victory on Northern soil. As an instinctive gambler, Lee also sensed that the victories at Fredericksburg and Chancellorsville offered the Confederacy one last chance to seize its own independence and bring in foreign powers; a defensive campaign could never provide such conditions. Jefferson Davis convened a series of meetings in May 1863 to discuss future strategy. Lee's powerful advocacy carried much weight with Davis's cabinet. Yet Vicksburg was under siege, and voices pleaded for its relief. The west did not lack military strength; what it lacked was organization and, even more, a directing brain. Davis agreed to support Lee's invasion but did not concentrate sufficiently to make it a truly powerful thrust; in particular, Davis ignored Lee's suggestion that Beauregard be put in command of another army on his right to guard his flank.

Apart from the cavalry action at Brandy Station (9 June) when Union troopers had almost worsted Stuart, the invasion of the North began brilliantly. The Army of Northern Virginia swept all before it in the Shenandoah Valley. The death of Jackson had forced Lee to reorganize his army, which he had divided into three smaller corps plus the cavalry. Stuart was given discretionary orders to attack Union communications in Maryland with more than half his command. It was not so much the cavalry but Stuart's talents that would be missed during the battle of Gettysburg, as two of Lee's corps commanders were inexperienced at that level of command.

As for Lee's opponents, Hooker remained in command but seemed at a loss as to what to do; he thought he might strike at Lee's communications just at the time when Lee had decided to do away with them and live off the country. In brief, Lee was experimenting with methods that would later be used much more brutally by William T. Sherman. Hooker then quarrelled with Halleck and was relieved on 28 June, being replaced by George G. Meade. Professorial in appearance, gentlemanly and thorough, Meade had an unenviable task. He was hurled into high command at a point of crisis and he, as yet, lacked moral authority over his subordinates. His lack of confidence was revealed in marked irritability.

Hill was making for Harrisburg when the division of Henry Heth collided with John Buford's brigade of cavalry near the town of Gettysburg. The clash drew in more units in a classic meeting engagement. Lee responded purely opportunistically, as was his wont, and without proper reconnaissance. He allowed himself to be drawn into a great battle and had to improvise a plan. Moving through Gettysburg, Lee's troops drove two Union corps back on to the high ground. Meade's corps moved slowly on to the ridges running southwards, the position resembling a fish hook. Lee sought to move

GETTYSBURG – PHASE I

The axes of military operations shift from north–south to east–west as Lee attempts to envelop the high ground south of Gettysburg. Union troops are driven out of the town and fortify the ridges. Meade orders a concentration and his corps move on to Cemetery Ridge and occupy the Little and Big Round Tops in the nick of time, thus anchoring the position securely. Lee attacks the centre, hoping to destroy Union corps piecemeal but the line holds.

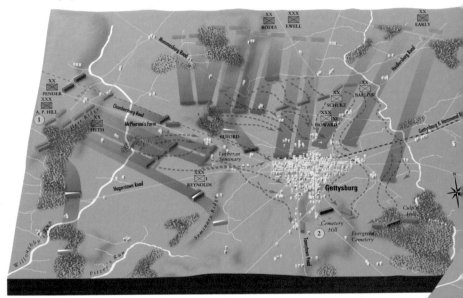

1. 1 July 5.30 am: Confederate forces drive Federal cavalry out of Gettysburg, and occupy the town

2. 4 pm: Federal troops fall back on Cemetery Hill and Culp's Hill and begin entrenching. By 6 pm Sickles corp arrives to strengthen the Federal force

3. 2 July from 4 pm: Confederates attack weakly held Federal left. Their attacks are successful but they are held at Little Round Top

4. to 5.30 pm: the struggle for the wheat field rages all day. The field changes hands four times and eventually the Federals are driven to the base of Little Round Top

5. 6.30 pm to dark: Confederates attack Cemetery Hill and Culp's Hill, but suffer severe losses and are unable to move the entrenched Federals

6. Federal reinforcements continue to arrive

rapidly, draw Meade's attention to the north, and then with a concentrated blow to the south break into Meade's position and destroy his corps piecemeal as they advanced towards Gettysburg. The plan was a perfectly good one, but it demanded urgent implementation.

Yet Lee did not receive the loyal co-operation that he had come to expect. The long concave position that his army occupied made co-ordination of the three corps difficult and cohesive movement kept breaking down. Meade had decided to fight but distributed a document known as the Pipe Creek Circular, detailing a position in Maryland to

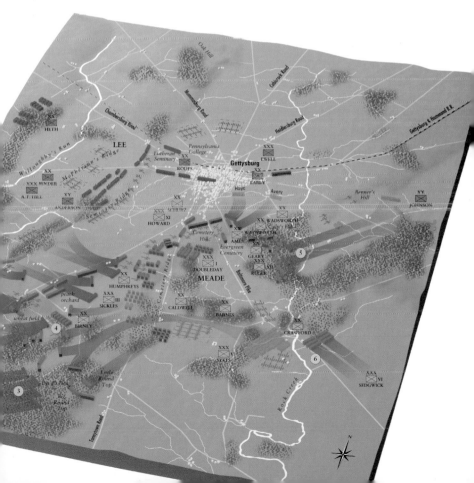

which the Army of the Potomac could withdraw should circumstances dictate retreat. Meade was a skilled tactician but tended to lack initiative; true to the spirit of the army, he was happiest on the defensive, content to jig to Lee's hornpipe.

On 2 July Longstreet's First Corps struck Meade's right. The terrain was undulating arable land without the thick woods that Lee had used to such advantage at Chancellorsville. The strength of Longstreet's blow was augmented by the decision of Daniel E. Sickles, the raffish commander of III Corps, to advance further forward from Cemetery

Meade's centre on 2 July, which held, thanks to the endurance of Northern troops. Horace Porter records that after the fighting stopped, men 'would start at the slightest sounds, and dodge at the flight of a bird or a pebble tossed at them'.

XX
ANDERSON

Seminary Ridge

XX
SCHUR

XX
TRIMBLE

XXX
XI
HOWARD

XX
PETTIGREW

3

XX
PICKETT

5

XX
GIBBON

Cemetery Ridge

Emmitsburg Road

4

XXX
I
DOUBLEDAY
(clts)

Peach
Orchard

XX
CALDWELL

Emmitsburg Road

GETTYSBURG – PHASE II

Lee renews the attack in the centre, calculating that a diversion would draw Meade's attention and resources to the north. 'Pickett's Charge' is then thrown forward, although Pickett's division of Virginians was only one element of the attacking force. However, the heated controversy among Southerners over responsibility for the defeat obscures the reality that it was won just as much by Northern efforts as by Southern errors.

THE YEAR OF TRIAL AND HOPE, 1862–3

1 3 July, 5.30 am–10 am: Johnson's division attacks Culp's Hill. Despite several attempts to seize the hill all are unsuccessful

2 1 pm: a massive artillery barrage begins, focused on Cemetery Ridge, and lasts for almost two hours

3 3 pm: Pickett's, Pettigrew's and half of Trimble's divisions led by Gen. Pickett advance toward Union positions

4 3.30 pm: a Federal brigade under Stannard attacks the flank of Pickett's division

5 3.45 pm: raked by Federal artillery, then musketry at close range, the Confederate survivors closed with Federal units, only to be driven back with many losses

6 5.30 pm: a Federal cavalry attack against the Confederate right flank is driven off

Ridge into the Peach Orchard, without explaining his move to Meade. The result was a limited Confederate success that drove Sickles's men back, but not the psychologically shattering blow that Lee hoped for. He decided to try again on 3 July, but by then Meade's position was greatly strengthened by breastworks. The Union artillery (354 guns to Lee's 272) was ready to concentrate its fire on attacking Confederate infantry.

Although the first two days of Gettysburg had witnessed Confederate successes, the third ended with a disastrous repulse. A diversionary attack on Cemetery Hill broke down, so Meade could give his full attention to the centre. The assault by elements of Longstreet's and Hill's Corps, immortalized by later apologists as 'Pickett's Charge', degenerated into an unsupported frontal charge which was thrown back by powerful artillery fire directed by Henry J. Hunt, who understood that the true role of cannon was as infantry-killers. Union infantry, standing behind breastworks, drove back the Confederate

Union dead at Gettysburg, the bodies already becoming bloated in the summer heat. Union fatalities numbered 3,063 and Confederate 3,903. Casualties totalled 51,053. It took many weeks to clear the field. Many bodies were placed in temporary graves to stop disease spreading.

attackers who survived the artillery barrage of round shot and canister with volleys of 'minnie'.

Although urged by some subordinates to launch an immediate counter-attack, Meade decided to do nothing to hazard his victory. His casualties were considerable: 23,063 to Lee's 28,063. Meade had handled his force skilfully in defence. Lee withdrew into the Shenandoah Valley. True to the best traditions of McClellan, and to Lincoln's dismay, Meade was content to shepherd Lee back to Virginia, even when he was trapped by the floodwaters of the Potomac. Though it had not brought the war to an end, the battle of Gettysburg was decisive. It sapped Lee's offensive power and handed the initiative back to the Union. But Meade's conduct offered little hope that he could win the war. Lincoln needed a general of greater confidence and surer imagination. The summer of 1863 revealed such a man in the west.

The early months of 1863 saw Grant struggling in the Mississippi bayous north-west of Vicksburg. A direct assault on the city by Sherman the previous December had been thrown back at Chickasaw Bluffs. Grant faced insuperable logistical difficulties and insurmountable (or so the Confederates assumed) geographical obstacles. Roads were bad and railways few. The country was inhospitable, unhealthy and untamed. The Mississippi rose and fell unaccountably and the weather was hot and humid. Yet Grant persevered. Vicksburg was significant strategically because it lay on the only high ground on the banks of the Mississippi south of Memphis. The railway ran east via Jackson, Mississippi and then to Chattanooga and Knoxville, and then ran west to Shreveport, Louisiana. Vicksburg was a vital link between the Trans-Mississippi and the Atlantic seaboard. Its loss would allow the remaining Confederate strongholds on the Mississippi to be picked off, and the abundant foodstuffs of Texas and Louisiana would be lost.

Grant faced one other, human, obstacle, Congressman John A. McClernand. Grant found out from the newspapers that McClernand had been given authority to raise a 'legion' among his Democratic supporters in Illinois, and was to command an independent operation that would 'sweep down' to Vicksburg and take it. In the spring of 1863 the shadow of interference was cast over Grant's operations. Yet though McClernand was a professional politician, Grant outmanoeuvred him at every stage. He took command in the field himself, and while McClernand was distracted by an operation up the Arkansas river culminating in the battle of Arkansas Post (14 January 1863), Grant settled down to use every possible expedient to traverse the Mississippi and get his troops before Vicksburg. One way was water power, making full use of close co-operation with the US Navy. Another was his army's engineering skills. He hoped to build a navigable channel that would link the Mississippi, Yazoo and Tallahatchie rivers. Trees had to be cut under water, and moves through the forests that resembled jungle resulted in the men often being covered by showers of snakes. Perverse flooding drowned the canal scheme and prevented a further move towards a Confederate fortified levée, Fort Pemberton. Still Grant did not give up. He hoped to get through Steele's Bayou and seize Haynes Bluff. But this time the water level fell and the US Navy gunboats were stranded in the shallows; they were only saved by Sherman's dramatic, candlelit, midnight march. All these set-backs added to the chorus of spiteful criticism of Grant, but did not deflect him from his aim: what he would call years later in his *Personal Memoirs* 'the one great object, that of opening the Mississippi'.

Grant had recently been informed by the general-in-chief, Halleck, that it was now government policy 'to live upon the enemy's country as much as possible and destroy his supplies. This is cruel warfare but the enemy has brought it upon himself by his own conduct'. He decided to turn the Confederate left, move down the Mississippi, and perhaps link up with another Union column, commanded by Nathaniel P. Banks, advancing north from Baton Rouge towards Grand Gulf. This was Lincoln's preferred course, but it was more cautious than the one that Grant eventually took. Because communication with Banks was haphazard, Grant decided to rely on his own resources, move south beyond Grand Gulf and then cross the Mississippi and advance into the hinterland south-east of Vicksburg – thus abandoning his own lines of communication. A simultaneous cavalry raid, commanded by Colonel Benjamin H. Grierson, set out from Tennessee to strike at Confederate communications; this drew away cavalry that would otherwise have been looking for Grant.

The Confederate commander at Vicksburg, John C. Pemberton, was a renegade Pennsylvanian. His reputation stood high at this date, but geography rather than his own ability had done his job for him. When tested he showed a fatal tendency to presume that Grant would do what he wanted him to do. Once securely across the Mississippi, Grant moved on a broad front of three corps, exploiting the fatal hesitancy of the Confederate command system. Johnston, the overall departmental commander, declined to take responsibility for the operations of his subordinates, and his boorish manner towards Davis verged on the irresponsible. Grant feinted towards Vicksburg to persuade Pemberton that the city was his immediate target, when in fact he was simply covering a deeper movement to seize the state capital, Jackson, and cut Pemberton's communications to the east. Johnston, with 10,000 men, was driven away from Jackson and was forced to try and relieve Vicksburg from the north-east. On 6 May Grant re-united his corps and began to advance on Vicksburg from the east. Pemberton actually outnumbered Grant. His total force consisted of 61,000 men to Grant's 43,000. But the further Grant advanced, the more distracted Pemberton became and the more his force was dispersed, so that Grant invariably contrived to gain a local superiority where it counted. Pemberton hurried to confront him at Champion's Hill, east of Vicksburg, but was utterly outmanoeuvred; but for an error by McClernand, Grant might have annihilated him and entered Vicksburg instantly.

Johnston urged Pemberton to evacuate Vicksburg and move north towards him; but Pemberton had received strict orders from Davis not to evacuate the city and he was not of a mind to disobey them. Johnston was absolutely right to urge concentration on Pemberton in order to break the cycle of dispersal that Grant had imposed on the Confederates. But Grant acted too quickly for him and invested Vicksburg on 19 May. He immediately assaulted the town hoping to exploit Confederate demoralization. He was persuaded by a misleading message from McClernand to continue the attack. Once he was sure that Vicksburg would not fall, he settled down to besiege the city and systematically advanced his trenchline, digging mines under Pemberton's defences. Two were exploded on 25 June and 1 July. The capitulation of Pemberton was only a matter of time, and he surrendered Vicksburg on 4 July. Port Hudson followed on 8 July. The Union at last enjoyed untrammelled communications along the Mississippi river.

The Confederate defeat at Gettysburg and the fall of Vicksburg ushered in a lull in the western and Virginian theatres, but activity increased in Tennessee. On 20 August William S. Rosecrans began his summer campaign designed to liberate East Tennessee by strategic

Union dug-outs at Vicksburg. Both the Confederate defences and the Union siege works were hurriedly improvised. The dug-outs are well placed to exploit the shade cast by the trees. In his Personal Memoirs, *Grant praised the ingenuity of his troops, who were never stymied by nature's challenges.*

movement. By the beginning of September Tullahoma had been occupied and Rosecrans's advance guard had entered Chattanooga. But Bragg's army had not been injured by these manoeuvres and he planned a counterstroke. Psychologically, Rosecrans was still thinking of the pursuit and his three corps were strung out over a front of 25–30 miles. Bragg's army was concentrated and would have trapped George H. Thomas's XIV Corps in McLemore's Cove but for the insubordination of his subordinates. A similar opportunity was missed on 12 September. Rosecrans had had a lucky escape and the three corps of the Army of the Cumberland were pulled together west of Chickamauga Creek. Here Bragg intended to attack.

The lull on the Virginia front had enabled the Confederate government to send Longstreet's Corps, minus its horses and artillery, by the ramshackle railway network, via Atlanta, to reinforce the Army of Tennessee. It was hoped that this would allow Bragg to inflict a truly decisive defeat on Rosecrans, drive him back and permit a reoccupation of central Tennessee. It was characteristic of Bragg's foolhardy and careless management of battles that he attacked Rosecrans prematurely on 19 September in a series of piecemeal and wasteful assaults. Longstreet arrived that night and was informed by Bragg that he intended to re-organize his army into two wings: Leonidas Polk would command the right, and Longstreet the left. He then told Longstreet that he would fix Rosecrans with the left and strike at the decisive point – the right – and cut him off from his communications to Chattanooga. Yet it was typical of Bragg's lack of method that this was a sector where his forces were weakest – only one division was available for the hammer blow on Rosecrans's left flank – and he entrusted the most important mission to a general – Polk – in whom he had no confidence. His orders were also vague, spelling out no precise tasks, only a series of movements to various locations. Not surprisingly, the battle turned out completely differently to Bragg's expectations.

At a Union council of war convened that night by Rosecrans, a consensus developed that the main Confederate attack would come on the Union left. Rosecrans shuffled his divisions northwards to defend the roads to Chattanooga. Rosecrans, like Bragg, tended to overwork, and having hardly slept that night he was overwrought. His line was strengthened by breastworks of logs and railway timbers but he lacked a reserve. The attack, delayed by at least two hours, began on the right, Polk's infantry throwing themselves against the breastworks of Thomas's troops. The Union artillery had a clear field of fire once the Confederates emerged from the woods and they were driven back in confusion.

Bragg's concept of attack as a series of synchronized blows, one following after another, too easily degenerated, because of a lack of detailed staff work, into intermittent assaults that could be driven back successively. But then fate intervened to present Longstreet with a great opportunity. If he had attacked in tandem with Polk he would have faced a strong, cohesive Union defence; but by the time he moved forward at 11 a.m., thanks to a muddle over a misunderstood order, a Union division moved out of line leaving a gaping hole on the right. Longstreet had aligned his infantry in a thick column to reduce the target offered to artillery, and this force plunged into Rosecrans's defences, shattering his right flank, and the centre soon followed suit and dissolved. The roads were choked with panic-stricken troops, Rosecrans at their head, racing back to Chattanooga. A pursuit on the left had never been planned; Longstreet sat down and consumed his lunch. Instead of masking Thomas's XIV Corps, which maintained a defensive line to the north,

1   20 September, 9.30 am–10 am: After delays, Confederate forces attack, only to be repulsed by heavy fire from Federal units

2   11 am–12 noon: Rosecrans mistakenly moves a Federal unit towards Kelly's Field and Confederate forces under Longstreet immediately advance through the gap created

3   Rosecrans moves units to the north. Meanwhile the right flank is overrun and the survivors flee. The exception is Wilder's brigade of mounted infantry which counter-attacks

4   Major-General George Thomas rallies Federal units into a line around Snodgrass Hill. Here they beat off repeated attacks, supported by the timely arrival of a fresh division

5   5.30 pm: After dark Thomas withdraws from Snodgrass Hill and Kelly's Field towards McFarland's Gap and Rossville. Federal forces are badly mauled but unbeaten. The Confederates are too exhausted for pursuit

CHICKAMAUGA

The Army of Tennessee's only victory, Chickamauga proved the validity of Tolstoy's dictum about battle in War and Peace *that 'For the most part things happened contrary to their orders'. Bragg had hoped to envelop Rosecrans's right, but the breakthrough came on the left because of a Union error. But the pursuit was laggardly and the opportunity to destroy the Army of the Cumberland was missed.*

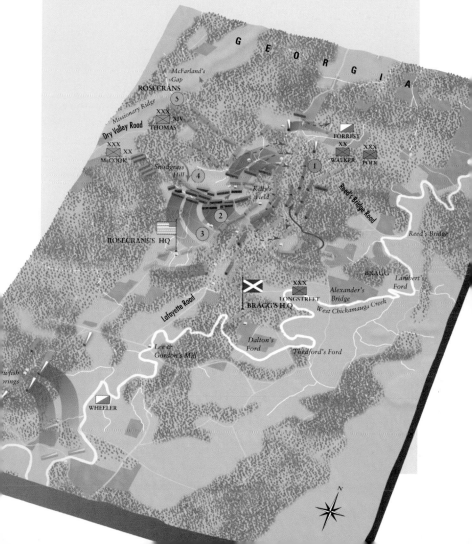

and pursuing Rosecrans back to Chattanooga, precious time and lives were wasted in spasmodic Confederate assaults on Snodgrass Hill, a position of no real operational significance. Thomas's men withdrew in good order the following day. The chance to take Chattanooga by a *coup de main* had been lost.

Chattanooga was then besieged. Chickamauga had been a great victory; indeed it was the only victory of the Army of Tennessee. It had been very costly: Bragg sustained 16,986 casualties, 25 per cent of the force engaged; Rosecrans lost 11,413 casualties and 8,000 prisoners. Despite this success the fruits of the battle were thrown away by a frenzied bout of internecine warfare among Bragg's generals, many of whom called for his dismissal. The fracas required the presence of the Confederate president to sort out. Bragg was sustained in his position, his friends were advanced, and Longstreet (one of the main troublemakers) was sent off to retake Knoxville. This major distraction depressed Confederate morale and allowed the Union to build up Chattanooga's defences.

In the meantime, Rosecrans was relieved and Grant dispatched to Chattanooga to take command of all Union forces in the west. Hooker was given command of two corps of the Army of the Potomac and sent to Tennessee; superior Union railways could more than match any Confederate concentration. When Grant arrived the garrison was starving and he immediately opened a supply line to the west. Once this was achieved, William T. Sherman and the Army of Tennessee arrived from Jackson, Mississippi, having lived off the land and destroyed the property of any recalcitrant rebels they came across. It would be good practice for the following year.

Bragg had never fought a defensive battle before and he greatly overestimated the strength of his position. His right ran along the narrow Missionary Ridge and his left was anchored on Lookout Mountain. Grant's original plan was to move Sherman's troops secretly to the left, then cross the Tennessee river and strike at the very edge of Bragg's right on Tunnel Hill. Thomas and a revived Army of the Cumberland was to demonstrate in the centre, and Hooker's role was enlarged (at Thomas's urging) to seize Lookout Mountain and then move on to the road centre at Rossville to cut Confederate communications. Grant's experience was very similar to Bragg's at Chickamauga; the battle turned out to be quite different to what he had expected. Where Grant differed from Bragg was that he had the flexibility to exploit his opportunities and the good sense to adapt his plan accordingly.

Hooker took Lookout Mountain, but Sherman's advance was held up by an error in identifying Tunnel Hill and then by the unexpectedly stubborn resistance put up by Patrick Cleburne's Division – one of the best fighting formations in the entire Confederate Army. Thomas's diversionary move in the centre around Orchard Knob inadvertently became the point of main effort when his men drove Confederate infantry out of the rifle pits at the bottom of Missionary Ridge. Then, carried away by the exhilaration of the moment, the troops continued their charge up Missionary Ridge itself. Confederate defenders could not fire on them for fear of hitting their own men; the ridge, moreover, was too steep for Confederate gunners to depress their gun barrels, and the top was too narrow to provide a strong fighting platform. Thomas's 23,000 men surged over its top and along its crest, completely rolling up Bragg's position. Bragg had no choice but to fall back on Dalton, Georgia. Bragg offered his resignation, and to his chagrin, it was immediately accepted.

The year 1863 had been one of contrasting fortunes. The Confederacy had won two important victories at Chancellorsville and at Chickamauga, both negated by Union ripostes at Gettysburg and Chattanooga. These successes laid the foundations for an eventual Union victory. In addition, the fall of Vicksburg had split the Confederacy in two, fulfilling the concept of the 'Anaconda Plan'. Tactically 1863 was significant because increased firepower substantially strengthened the defensive. Yet the indecisive outcome of many battles owed as much to weaknesses in command and organization as to improvements in weapons technology. Every great battle fought in 1863, from

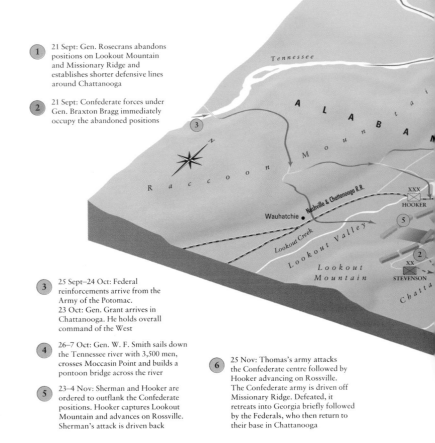

1 21 Sept: Gen. Rosecrans abandons positions on Lookout Mountain and Missionary Ridge and establishes shorter defensive lines around Chattanooga

2 21 Sept: Confederate forces under Gen. Braxton Bragg immediately occupy the abandoned positions

3 25 Sept–24 Oct: Federal reinforcements arrive from the Army of the Potomac. 23 Oct: Gen. Grant arrives in Chattanooga. He holds overall command of the West

4 26–7 Oct: Gen. W. F. Smith sails down the Tennessee river with 3,500 men, crosses Moccasin Point and builds a pontoon bridge across the river

5 23–4 Nov: Sherman and Hooker are ordered to outflank the Confederate positions. Hooker captures Lookout Mountain and advances on Rossville. Sherman's attack is driven back

6 25 Nov: Thomas's army attacks the Confederate centre followed by Hooker advancing on Rossville. The Confederate army is driven off Missionary Ridge. Defeated, it retreats into Georgia briefly followed by the Federals, who then return to their base in Chattanooga

Murfreesboro to Chattanooga, was, however, fought over two or three days. With the industrial capacity to sustain fighting over longer periods, and the means to supply armies from their factories, both sides now geared themselves up for even more bloody encounters in 1864. Yet the influence of industrial capacity favoured the North over the South. The Northern economy was galvanized by the civil war. By 1865 federal expenditure had risen to 3.4 billion dollars. Tax revenue amounted to only 22 per cent of the total, the rest coming from 'greenbacks' that could be converted into government bonds. By August 1865 the net federal wartime debt had risen to 2.8 billion dollars, almost one half of the Gross National Product (GNP).

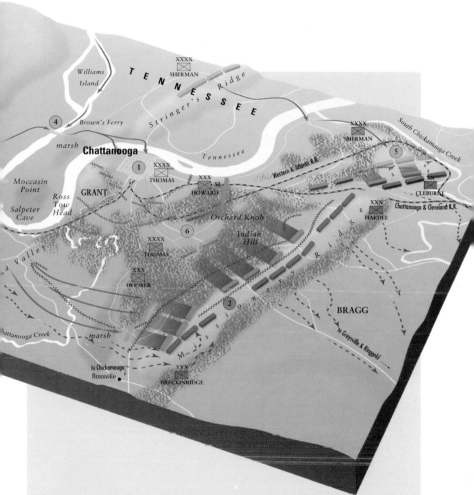

CHATTANOOGA SEPT–OCT 1863

Grant had intended using Sherman's Army of the Tennessee to strike Bragg's right, and he was moved across the Tennessee river to Tunnel Hill, using the terrain to screen his movements. Hooker struck Bragg's left on Lookout Mountain. But Sherman was held up, and without orders, Thomas's men from the Army of the Cumberland surged up Missionary Ridge and breached Bragg's defences, which were weaker than he had calculated.

CHAPTER FOUR

The Civil War: Confederate Collapse 1864–5

Unkempt and rather scruffy, Sherman typified
a new breed of Union generals that had risen
to the top by 1864. He was energetic, incredibly
restless and vigorous. In 1864 he wrote, 'I
propose to demonstrate the vulnerability of
the South and make its inhabitants feel that
war and individual ruin are synonymous
terms.' A brilliant artist of manoeuvre, though
Sherman never lost a campaign, he never
actually directed a victory in a pitched battle.

Confederate Collapse, 1864–5

GRANT'S VICTORY AT Chattanooga ushered in a lull in the two most important theatres of operations, Tennessee and Virginia, as both sides licked their wounds and busied themselves with preparations for the next campaign. There was then a period of strategic rationalization, rather like that following First Manassas. In February 1864 Congress passed a bill enabling Grant to receive the rank of lieutenant general. Only George Washington had held this commission previously (Winfield Scott's was a brevet). The act conferred on Grant a prestige so impressive that he could ignore the Joint Committee on the Conduct of the War, even though its members were not counted among the growing number of his admirers. Shortly afterwards Grant was appointed general-in-chief. Sherman had urged on him the desirability of staying out of Washington and directing all operations from the west. After his first visit to the capital, Grant realized that such a course was impracticable. Virginia was the centre of gravity of the war and President Lincoln would not have sanctioned his absence from it. At last Lincoln had found his general, and thereafter Grant was the directing head of the Union war effort, although he was far from being an all-powerful generalissimo. Grant's power rested on four parallel foundations: the confidence of the president and the close coincidence in their strategic views; the military prestige accruing from his previous victories, which afforded him a strong moral authority that his predecessors in Virginia had lacked; the power to issue orders to the heads of the staff bureaux in Washington (the chief engineer, the quartermaster-general, etc.), a power that the Secretary of War had previously denied; finally, his intention to command armies in the field, not sit in an office in Washington, as Halleck had done to universal ridicule.

By shrewd judgement Grant had done much to solve the command problem that had dogged McClellan. He decided not to command the Army of the Potomac himself, thus easing his workload, but he intended to travel with it as a kind of superior army commander. This was the level of command that his contemporaries identified with military operations, and Grant thus identified himself with it. Meade was confirmed in command of the Army of the Potomac although his position was unenviable given the close proximity of Grant. Halleck was confirmed in the position of chief of staff and attended to much of the administrative and organizational work that supported the armies. His part in the final Union victory was far from insignificant. Sherman succeeded to Grant's position as commander of the Military Division of the Mississippi. Although Grant's brisk and dynamic presence did

When Charles Francis Adams, Jr., saw Grant in the Wilderness in May 1864, he thought him 'a very ordinary looking man'. Actually, Grant was a superb horseman, and graceful in an under-stated way. He was modest, self-effacing, but utterly imperturbable. He was remorseless in pursuit of his object.

much to galvanize the Union war effort he did not revolutionize it. The 1864 changes were much stronger in terms of improving the organization of the Union war effort and preparing armies for war than in the actual conduct of operations. Grant did not preside over a great general staff, and the system relied heavily on the lubrication provided by personal friendship, especially between Grant and Sherman. Indeed Grant's staff never exceeded fifteen officers, and relations between it and Meade's staff were marked by friction and overlap. Grant's device of a dual-headed system of command was inefficient but, given the political realities that constrained him, probably unavoidable.

The process of modernization, in other words, evinced by the American Civil War should not be exaggerated. The influence of the political process also explains why Union and Confederate armies remained smaller than many of the armies raised during the Napoleonic

George G. Meade and his staff in 1864. Meade disappeared from public view in 1864 after he punished a war correspondent, Edward Cropsey, who had published an insulting article. Cropsey was put on a mule with placards proclaiming 'Libeller of the Press'. Thereafter Meade was excised from all news stories.

Wars and in the Prussian Wars of Unification. The total number of soldiers raised by the Union alone exceeded 2 million, yet the field armies were quite small by nineteenth-century standards. The largest Union army was the Army of the Potomac, which had a maximum strength of 'effectives' of 130,000 men during the Chancellorsville campaign. The armies raised by Moltke in Prussia were far larger. The reasons for this are twofold: the methods by which the armies were raised, and the way in which they were employed. Given the strength of the American political tradition with its hostility to all forms of institutionalized, government-sponsored military organization (as opposed to local, which had a wide measure of support), the structure of the regular army was set aside during the Civil War. Initially, at least, recruiting was the province of the state political apparatus. Again, this is not surprising because the organization of the Republican party in 1861–2 was far more sophisticated and centralized than the federal government. States were responsible for raising the men and putting them into uniform, the federal authorities for training and equipping them with weapons.

The soldiers raised were a mix of volunteers whose enthusiasm had subsided by the autumn of 1862 and those raised by the draft. The volunteers served for a fixed time period with no guarantee that they would re-enlist. Consequently, there was a high turnover of men entering and leaving the army when their enlistments expired. Whole regiments were denuded of their men and entirely new ones raised, thus dissipating experience. By the spring of 1863 the North faced a severe manpower shortage. Congress passed the Enrolment Act of March 1863 to solve it, but this legislation was very far from representing a rational manpower policy. Four drafts raised 776,000; the first provoked the New York Draft Riots in the summer of 1863, and no fewer than three drafts were required to fill up the quotas which were completed by lottery. An elaborate process of exemptions, commutation fees and the payment of substitutes ensured that only a small percentage of any group ended up in the ranks of the army. Such a system favoured the wealthy; immigrants were keen to serve as substitutes. Of 207,000 men who were drafted in 1864 only 46,000 went into the army. In total half a billion dollars were spent on finding substitutes. The Confederacy had a better record in organizing its limited manpower. In April 1862 it passed a Conscription Act which made all white men between the ages of 18 and 35 liable for military service, permitted some occupational exemptions but outlawed substitutes. However, this system too was subject to abuses. One source of fighting men that was turned to reluctantly but, in the event, proved essential, was American blacks. By 1865, 186,000 blacks had served in the US Army, and even the Confederacy considered arming slaves in its last desperate days.

The raising of black troops was initially unpopular. One private of the 89th Illinois wrote after the Battle of Nashville, 'I have often he[a]rd men say that they would not fight beside a Negro soldier but ... whites and blacks charged together and they fell just as well as we did ...'

The methods by which these armies were raised profoundly influenced the manner in which they were deployed. The great extent of the Civil War led to a diffusion of strength to cover a great variety of commitments and garrisons. These, in turn, reduced the pool of manpower available for the field armies. Ambitious and influential politicians who held generals' commissions were mollified and their loyalty guaranteed (especially if they were Democrats) by offers of their own commands; this accentuated the tendency towards dispersal. But the most important reason that American armies remained smaller than European was the fluidity of the pool of manpower, with men moving in and out of the army at any one moment. For example, a significant proportion of the three-year volunteers engaged in July 1861 left the army in the middle of the 1864 campaign.

Grant was urged to simplify the recruiting process but did not, calculating that the Northern margin of superiority was just enough to ensure victory. Once Grant stopped the effective exchange of prisoners based on parole – which favoured the South – he managed to secure that room for manoeuvre on the manpower front which would render massive Northern superiority in the field.

The soldiers themselves were not easy to command. They were convinced of their rights and often regarded themselves as just civilians in uniform. They had strong opinions and did not fear to express them. Earlier in the war they were often commanded by political leaders who gave their constituents rousing speeches. In both Union and Confederate armies soldiers initially elected their officers and NCOs, which led to popularity contests rather than the imposition of military discipline. By the end of 1862 this had died out and incompetent officers were rooted out by Commissions Boards. The soldiers were young – the average age of a regiment would be about 24, though many men would be only 18–19 years old. By European standards the levels of literacy were very high, although illiteracy was higher in the Confederacy. Matters had to be explained to the soldiers; their blind adherence could not be relied upon. Generals like Don Carlos Buell who were not natural leaders with striking, extrovert personalities were dismissed as 'martinets'. An informal system of discipline often worked best. Not for nothing did the great Southern historian Douglas Southall Freeman describe the Army of Northern Virginia as a 'voluntary association'.

Soldiers on both sides took a close interest in the issues raised by the war, not least the protection of America's cherished democratic experiment which was regarded as a beacon for the rest of mankind. Some were exercised by the racial issues of the war and wished to end slavery. At first this tended to be a minority view, mainly held by middle-class intellectuals. Most soldiers were opposed to the Emancipation Proclamation when it was issued. But the further Northern armies penetrated into the Southern heartland, the more the soldiers realized that the Southern war economy rested upon slavery, and the more enthusiastic they became to see its extirpation. As for Southerners, their sense of nationalism was much cruder, although the Army of Northern Virginia witnessed a rise of aggressive Confederate nationalism, as opposed to state particularism, especially among its young company-level officers. Given the number of severe set-backs the South had suffered since the summer of 1863, a religious revival flourished among the ranks of the Confederacy's armies – perhaps as a source of solace and inspiration for greater perseverance.

Morale tended to oscillate between extremes, and emotions were fanned by newspapers, which enjoyed a wide circulation in military camps. An earlier fastidiousness about protecting Southern property had quickly disappeared. It was replaced by a consensus that the South should be punished for bringing war to a peaceful country; living off the country led to depredations and mindless destruction. It was this attitude that Sherman was to exploit in the autumn of 1864. Yet the looseness of military discipline encouraged desertion. Some deserters were simply bored by the tedium of camp life – that was in poor contrast to the romantic notions that men had been fed when the war began. The size of the country and the scale of the operations

This photograph (originally a 3¼ inch by 3½ inch ambrotype that could be made in minutes and sold cheaply) is of Private E. J. Jennison from Georgia. He was killed at Malvern Hill in 1862 aged 16. The minimum age for recruitment was 18, but boys often lied about their ages.

meant that it was very difficult to supervise soldiers, and absconding was easy; sometimes entire units deserted, together with their officers. The number of deserters was huge. In February 1865 it was calculated that the Union Army had 338,536 absentees (with 630,924 present for duty), while the Confederate Army had 194,494 absentees (and only 160,198 present for duty). Admittedly, not all absentees were deserters, but the numbers were high. Draconian punishments did little to stop the haemorrhaging from the ranks. Lincoln tended to prevent widespread shooting of deserters. In 1864 he intervened to prevent the execution of the son of the American minister to Prussia; but the sons of the humbler families were also the recipients of presidential compassion. The true significance of the chaotic manpower policy, indiscipline in the ranks and the high levels of desertion, lay in the measure of American unpreparedness to meet the challenges of war in the industrial age.

Grant's intention was to finish the war in the spring of 1864. He hoped to be in possession of the Confederate capital by the end of May. He intended to organize a simultaneous advance on every front to distract Confederate armies and weaken their ability to concentrate their forces. Sherman, with three armies under his command, was to advance on Atlanta, Georgia. Grant himself was to supervise the advance of three armies in Virginia. The Army of the Potomac was to advance overland towards Richmond; Fritz Sigel was to advance down the Shenandoah Valley and cut Richmond's communications from the west; Benjamin F. Butler was to advance from the Bermuda Hundred, a meander in the James river, with the 30,000 men of the Army of the James, and cut Richmond's communications with the railway junction of Petersburg to the south of the Confederate capital. After much thought, Grant had decided to turn Lee's right flank and bring him to battle outside the Richmond defences. He had not fought Lee before and underestimated his skill in defence; many senior officers in the Army of the Potomac expected him to be crushed in the first round.

The Army of the Potomac crossed the Rapidan on 5 May 1864 and proceeded to march through the Wilderness, taking much the same route as Hooker had the year before. Grant was anxious to get through this congested area, but had issued orders to Meade that if an opportunity was found to 'pitch into' Lee's army then he should take it. Lee had not yet concentrated his army, and his three corps were scattered for subsistence. He was not anxious to bring on a battle until his army had reunited but was ready to contest the initiative, and hoped to smash Grant's right flank and force him back over the Rapidan. A Fabian scheme offered greater attraction in 1864 because the protracted process of selecting and electing a president would continue throughout the summer regardless of the war.

On 5 May a meeting engagement began on Lee's right before his concentration was complete. If Grant could get in an overwhelming blow before Longstreet could come up then the fragments of Lee's army would be shattered and the Union Army could enter Richmond. He ordered Meade to prepare a massive assault with Hancock's II Corps early the following morning. With Meade directing tactics, Grant remained at his headquarters in order, so a member of his staff, Horace Porter, explained, 'to be able to communicate more promptly with the different commands'. As the Army of the Potomac advanced, so telegraph lines were rapidly laid behind it. Hancock's attack early the following morning was a complete success. The Confederates had failed to entrench properly and were driven back in confusion towards the Widow Tapp's farm. A concerted Union attack in the centre, however, had failed to make any progress because of the tangled vegetation. Lee was given time to reorganize his shaky units, and then the dramatic news was announced that Longstreet's men had arrived. Surging through the woods, they smashed into Hancock's exposed left flank and drove his men back. Longstreet, like Jackson before him, was wounded as he went forward to order a pursuit, and the battle gradually came to an end.

Previously, after such set-backs the Army of the Potomac had withdrawn northwards. The following morning Grant ordered an advance to the south-east to Spotsylvania Court House. His order was greeted by cheers from the Union troops. But because of better discipline and initiative, Lee's troops managed to steal a march on

A deserted camp at Fredericksburg. The Army of the Potomac had attempted to push beyond the Rappahannock river – the Dare Mark – for two years before Grant's arrival in the east. The encampment shows just how permanent these quarters had become by 1864.

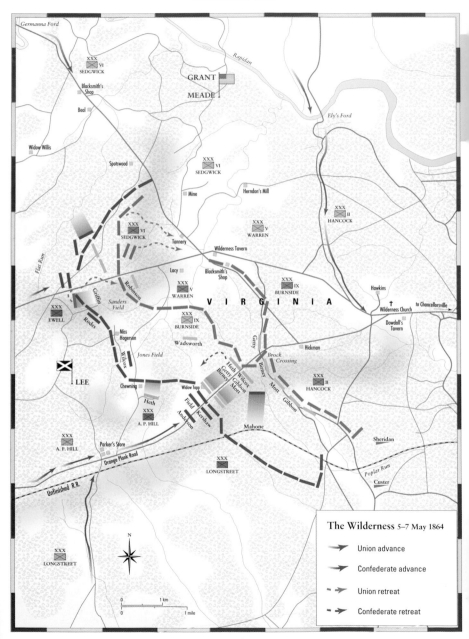

The Wilderness 5–7 May 1864

→ Union advance

→ Confederate advance

⇢ Union retreat

⇢ Confederate retreat

THE WILDERNESS

This battle was essentially a draw, as the respective attempts to outflank the Confederate right and the Union left failed. Yet Grant still held the initiative, and unlike those that had commanded before him, he was determined to make full use of it.

Meade's men, and on arrival immediately entrenched. Thanks to the lie of the high ground covering the crossroads, the Confederate breastworks developed into a vulnerable salient. Grant at once resolved to take the offensive, as he was determined to overcome the defensive mentality of the Army of the Potomac. He had, however, weakened his ability to strike at Lee in his home territory by dispatching Philip H. Sheridan and his cavalry off on another raid towards Richmond. This was more successful than Stoneman's the previous year, as Stuart's cavalry were defeated and their commander killed at Yellow Tavern on 12 May. Sheridan then successfully linked up with Butler, whose small force had been driven back to the safety of the Bermuda Hundred, before returning to Meade's lines. However, throughout the remainder of the campaign, Grant and Meade suffered from faulty intelligence and often had to guess what was in front of them. This did not deter Grant because he was anxious that Lee should not be allowed to dispatch reinforcements to Beauregard, who now commanded on the James riverfront, which could overwhelm the Army of the James. In any case, he misinterpreted Lee's use of entrenchments as a sign of faltering morale. Grant believed that another powerful blow would rout the Army of Northern Virginia. He took advantage of the absence of Lee's cavalry, preoccupied with chasing Sheridan, to shift his supply base to Port Royal on the Rappahannock, thus shortening his lines of supply.

The battle of Spotsylvania, 8–21 May, was an attritional slogging match of the most ferocious kind. The stakes were high on both sides, as the two great adversaries were determined to fight it out. Grant probed for an exposed flank before launching a massive attack on Lee's

SPOTSYLVANIA

This battle, spread over ten days, degenerated into an attritional slogging match. Grant threw in a series of attacks attempting to find a weak spot. Meade's tactical direction was handicapped by poor intelligence. With inspiring leadership, Lee held the line successfully. However, Grant retained the initiative and continued to move south-east towards Richmond.

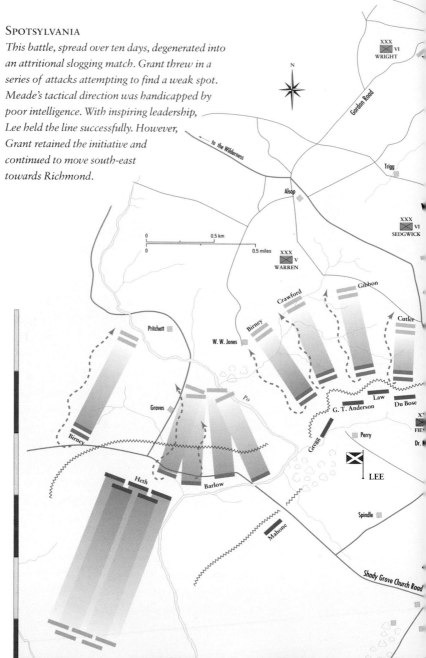

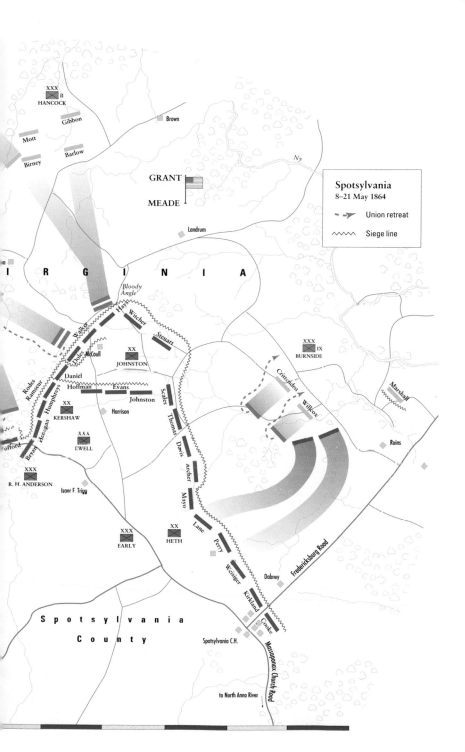

Spotsylvania
8–21 May 1864

- - → Union retreat
∿∿∿ Siege line

XXX II HANCOCK
Gibbon
Mott
Birney
Barlow
Brown

GRANT
MEADE

Landrum

V I R G I N I A

Bloody Angle
Walker Hays Witcher
Stuart
Doles McCoull
XX JOHNSTON
Daniel
Hoffman Evans
Johnston
Scales
Thomas
Davis
Archer
Mayo
Lane
Perry
Weisiger
Kirkland
Cooke
Rodes
Ramseur
Brig gen Humphreys
XX KERSHAW
Harrison
XXX EWELL
Bratt
offord
XXX R. H. ANDERSON
Isaac F. Trigg
XXX EARLY
XX HETH

XXX IX BURNSIDE
Crittenden
Willcox
Marshall
Ruins
Dabney
Fredericksburg Road

Spotsylvania County

Spotsylvania C.H.

Massaponax Church Road

to North Anna River

Ny

Trenches at Spotsylvania. The avalanche of projectiles fired by the rifled musket and artillery is forcing soldiers to 'dig in' throughout 1864. The trenches are shallow by comparison with those of 1914–15, but recourse is often had to abattis (foreground) and other obstructions.

left and centre in the late afternoon of 10 May. Colonel Emory Upton had actually thought out new tactics, based on the velocity of the assault and exploiting the undulating ground, and broke into the Confederate breastworks on the west side of the salient. But the tangled vegetation and thick woods made it difficult for Meade to see when and where breakthroughs had occurred and thus to order reserves forward to the correct point. The telegraph was no help under such conditions. Upton was not supported and Confederates rushed from other sectors of the front to drive him back. The following day Grant, aware of the need to reassure the administration, wrote Halleck a famous letter in which he stated that he intended to fight it out 'on this line if it takes all Summer'. Grant still thought in terms of a short campaign – though now of months rather than weeks. Grant and Meade believed that Lee's line had assumed a salient form, but they were very unclear as to what precisely this form had taken. Hancock was ordered to attack it but he, too, did not know where it was. By dint of good luck his corps of 20,000 men suddenly appeared out of the fog and rushed the weakest part of the line, taking its defenders completely by surprise. This was the point at which Grant should have won the battle, but simultaneous advances by neighbouring corps were ordered too late; Lee sealed off the penetration and ordered his men to hold their new line or die in the attempt. The fighting was frenzied and hand-to-hand. Confederate soldiers held their positions for twenty-four hours without refreshment. 'I am sure that Hell can't beat that terrible scene,' wrote one soldier.

Grant tried once more on 15 May and attacked frontally over the same ground in front of the salient, but the Confederate artillery took a terrible toll of his infantry, followed up by infantry volleys; only a handful of men reached the breastworks. On 21 May Grant called off his attempt to shatter Lee's army and moved once more around his flank. These battles are sometimes compared with the great battles of the Western Front in 1914–18. There are some similarities, not least the problem of how to deploy tactical reserves once a penetration of an entrenched line was effected. However, the battles of 1864–5 were much more open and artillery was, as yet, incapable of disposing of breastworks, thus driving their builders further underground. But the key feature of trench warfare, namely, fighting of savage intensity followed by periods of comparative quiet, was already present in these battles in Virginia.

After some skilful fencing on the Totopotomy Creek and North Anna river, Grant moved around to the right once more, with Lee keeping between him and Richmond. At Cold Harbor, on 3 June, Grant thought he had at last caught Lee outside his entrenchments and attacked in a badly managed offensive. Lee's men were safely behind their breastworks and the fields of fire were good. In his finest defensive victory since Fredericksburg, Lee inflicted a total of 7,000 casualties on Grant for trifling loss.

The siege works at Petersburg, which by the spring of 1865 came to resemble a sector of the Western Front in 1915. Grant's works consisted of deep trenches supported by earthwork forts at important points.

Grant decided that the only way to pull Lee out of his breastworks was to transfer his forces south of the James river and move on Petersburg from the south. As he had moved south-easterly, Grant was able to take advantage of the Union command of the sea. In a brilliantly conceived operation, he bridged the James river, linked up with Butler and advanced on Petersburg as planned. After the set-back at Cold Harbor, Grant's generals tended to move cautiously and stopped as soon as they faced breastworks. They lost the chance to take

SIEGE OF PETERSBURG

The siege of the railway junction of Petersburg on the Appomattox, a tributary of the James river, was the key to Richmond. Beauregard carried out a skilful defence, based on his mastery of swagger and bluff, before being superseded by Lee. Grant attempted to break through at 'the Crater' in July. After this disappointment, Grant gradually extended his lines westwards to stretch the Confederate defences to breaking point.

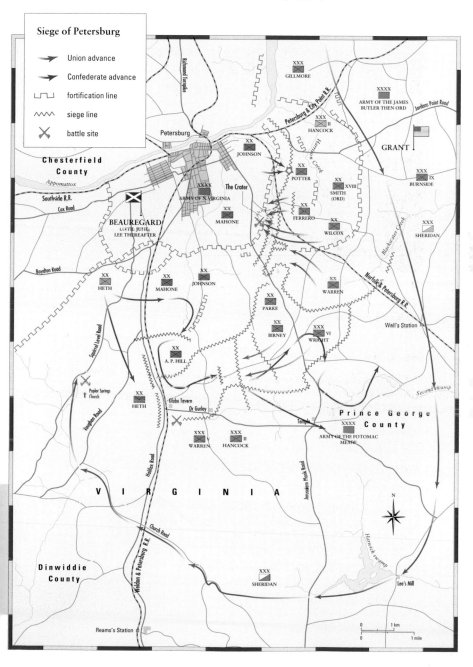

CONFEDERATE COLLAPSE, 1864–5

Petersburg before Lee transferred his troops to the south side and began digging in. Grant had no choice but to resort to siege tactics as he had at Vicksburg. In July he tried to break through by exploding a massive mine underneath the Confederate defences; unfortunately 'the Crater' was so impressive that the attacking troops crowded into it to stare in awe. Defenders shot at them 'like fish in a barrel' and the early success was transformed into a humiliating failure. Grant settled down before Petersburg to besiege it and elaborate fieldworks spread out for miles around. If Lee was held here, then Sherman could continue his advance into Georgia unmolested. The only distraction was Jubal Early's raid up the Shenandoah Valley which reached the outskirts of Washington on 11 July. Lincoln and other politicians were vexed lest he enter the city, but Grant sent the veterans of VI Corps to man the city's defences, and Sheridan was given command of the Army of the Shenandoah. Early was driven back by victories at Opequon Creek and Fisher's Hill, to be crushed finally at Cedar Creek on 19 October 1864. Sheridan was

Confederate prisoners of war captured by Philip Sheridan's troops at the Battle of Fisher's Hill, Virginia, are sent to the rear under the guard of Union troops. At this stage in the war, Grant had ended all exchanges of prisoners that had previously favoured the Confederacy.

ordered by Grant to 'Take all provisions, forage and stock wanted for the use of your command. Such as cannot be consumed, destroy.' Sheridan set about his task with enthusiasm and systematically destroyed the agricultural wealth of the Shenandoah Valley. With this ruthless action, the 1864 campaign in the east came to an end.

Grant had not consciously planned an attritional campaign in Virginia in the spring of 1864 but that was how it had turned out. These operations, however, had an important by-product. By pinning Lee to Richmond, he permitted Sherman to manoeuvre into the Confederate heartland. Sherman consistently sought to manoeuvre around the left flank of his opponent, Joseph E. Johnston. Sherman was much the more imaginative of the two, and in the main, the greater soldier. Johnston was pernickety and prudent to the point of over-caution; he was able in defence, being shrewd in his choice of position and economical in holding it; but he was too much of a perfectionist ever to risk an offensive movement. Consequently, unlike Lee he never contested the initiative and merely withdrew in the face of Sherman, continually abandoning territory when confronted with Union advances. Thus he played to Sherman's strong suit. Sherman was at his best when he was allowed the freedom to develop his imaginative manoeuvres; and this space Johnston abandoned to him. Sherman also commanded a host of other operations in the west. A series of smaller campaigns continued in the Trans-Mississippi in Arkansas, and Missouri was convulsed by guerrilla warfare. These operations were not unimportant, but the course of the war in the west was decided by the great movements in Georgia.

Sherman had three armies under his immediate command and he directed them as Grant did in the east by issuing orders to their commanders. His own former command, the Army of the Tennessee, was headed by James B. McPherson and fielded 25,000 men; the Army of the Cumberland of 60,000 men was headed by George H. Thomas, and John M. Schofield's Army of the Ohio had 13,000 men. Sherman's force had only a single rail track over which to carry supplies. He had to advance covering his rail link – an indication of the new vulnerabilities that the railway introduced. The terrain over which he moved was rough, sharp and irregular, riven by deep ravines, and eminently defensible. Johnston's Army of Tennessee had had the considerable benefit of its commander's organizational skills for almost six months, and its 65,000 men were well drilled and as refreshed as a Confederate army could be. He took up a strong position on the Rocky Face Ridge, daring Sherman to attack him. Sherman had no intention of doing so; he pinned Johnston to his position and sent his striking force, McPherson's Army of the Tennessee, on a wide envelopment through the unguarded Snake Creek Gap, to cut the railroad at Resaca. McPherson was too cautious and he pulled back before he had cut the railroad, thus allowing Johnston to escape when he withdrew on the night of 12/13 May. Sherman said to McPherson afterwards: 'Well, Mac, you missed the opportunity of your life.' Sherman was justified in this complaint but some of the blame was his, too. Before the operation began, Thomas suggested that the Army of the Cumberland should be given the outflanking role. Sherman thought Thomas (his old West Point room-mate) too ponderous and lacking in spark for a manoeuvre mission, and he favoured his old army rather too blatantly.

In an effort to locate a weak spot, Sherman sent McPherson towards the Oostanaula river to cut Johnston's rail communications with Atlanta. Johnston showed his customary skill in disengagement, and briefly contemplated launching a counterstroke before withdrawing to Cassville. The Davis administration was determined that Atlanta should be held. It was an important communications point, and although the town's population was small (only 20,000), it housed important iron foundries and granaries. Further, Johnston's Fabian delaying tactics were already causing the Davis administration political problems because the advance of Union troops led to the destruction of slavery; the slaves flocked to the Union lines, and their owners were out of pocket. The morale of Confederate troops was also adversely affected, and under pressure from Davis, Johnston decided to make a stand at Cassville. Sherman was advancing on a broad twelve-mile front, as was his wont. Johnston planned to concentrate two of his corps and strike the small force of Schofield, separated from Sherman's main body by seven miles. One of the corps commanders, John B. Hood, became alarmed over the security of his flanks, took fright and called the operation off. Johnston was forced to withdraw back through the Allatoona Pass to a new position behind the Etowah river, having missed the best opportunity of the campaign to launch a counterstroke. The irony was that it was Hood who had acted prudently. He had built his reputation in Virginia on audacity bordering on the foolhardy, and had been severely wounded twice. While convalescing after losing a leg at Chickamauga he had befriended the President and had begun writing to him detailing Johnston's inadequacies as an offensive commander.

Sherman began to move away from Allatoona, determined not to reduce the pressure on Johnston. He was aware of the great battles that Grant was fighting against Lee, and knew that they had not been as successful as Grant had hoped. He was determined to prevent Confederate reinforcements being sent from Georgia to succour Lee. He had managed to build up twenty days of supplies; swinging round Johnston's left, he advanced on the road junction at Dallas, lying in the thick woods twenty miles distant in Johnston's rear and only twenty miles from Atlanta. The Confederate cavalry discovered this movement in the nick of time, and as at Spotsylvania, on 25 May Johnston's units rushed to New Hope Church to block Sherman's advance. The fighting was sporadic and involved much skirmishing and sniping. During an artillery exchange Johnston and his generals showed themselves and Polk was killed (for all his tactical inadequacies, he had been a popular figure among the soldiers). The sheer physical pressure of the campaign, especially the intense fighting in the Georgia heat, wore down even the toughest men, and the great bulk of Sherman's casualties were from disease and mental exhaustion. To make matters worse, the rain poured down, turning the roads, mostly dusty tracks,

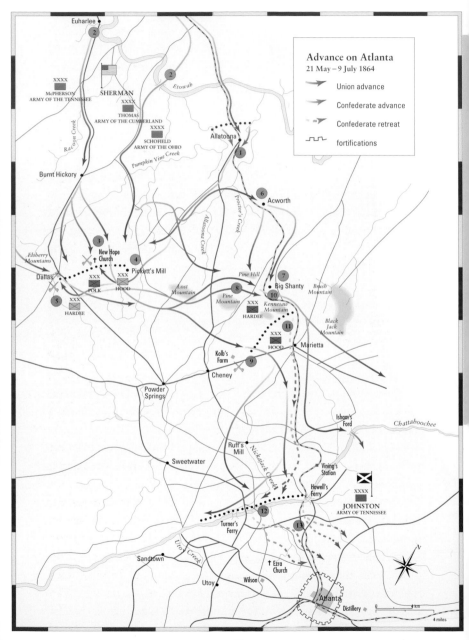

Advance on Atlanta
21 May – 9 July 1864

Union advance

Confederate advance

Confederate retreat

fortifications

Euharlee

2

SHERMAN

XXXX
McPHERSON
ARMY OF THE TENNESSEE

XXXX
THOMAS
ARMY OF THE CUMBERLAND

XXXX
SCHOFIELD
ARMY OF THE OHIO

Etowah

2

Allatoona

1

Raccoon Creek

Pumpkin Vine Creek

Burnt Hickory

Acworth

6

Allatoona Creek

Proctor's Creek

Elsberry Mountains

3

New Hope
Church

4

Pickett's Mill

Dallas

XXX
POLK

XXX
HOOD

5

XXX
HARDEE

Lost
Mountain

Pine
Mountain

8

Pine Hill

Big Shanty

7

Brush
Mountain

10

XXX
HARDEE

Kennesaw
Mountain

Black
Jack
Mountain

11

XXX
HOOD

Marietta

Kolb's
Farm

9

Cheney

Powder
Springs

Ruff's
Mill

Sweetwater

Nickajack Creek

Isham's
Ford

Chattahoochee

Vining's
Station

Howell's
Ferry

XXXX
JOHNSTON
ARMY OF TENNESSEE

Turner's
Ferry

12

13

Sandtown

Utoy Creek

Utoy

Wilson

† Ezra
Church

N

Atlanta

Distillery

0   4 km

0   4 miles

ADVANCE ON ATLANTA

Sherman's advance on Atlanta, May to July 1864, was a mentally and physically gruelling campaign, but Sherman held the initiative throughout. As he bypassed Johnston's defensive lines successively, Confederate resistance slackened. Indeed his troops faced 'such feeble resistance', he admitted in his Memoirs, 'that I really thought the enemy intended to evacuate the place'. He was wrong: the campaign would last another two months.

1 20–21 May: Johnston places army in position impregnable to frontal attack at Allatoona

2 23–24 May: Sherman crosses the Etowah in two columns and advances toward Marietta

3 25 May: Johnston blocks Sherman's flanking move at Dallas and New Hope Church

4 27 May: Howard tries to turn Johnston's right flank at Pickett's Mill but is repulsed

5 28 May: Hardee's corps and Armstrong's cavalry brigade bungle attack on the XV Corps east of Dallas

6 31 May–6 June: Sherman falls back to Acworth and railroad

7 10–19 June: Sherman advances through rain and mud to area north and west of Kennesaw Mountain

8 12 June: Polk killed on Pine Mountain

9 22 June: Hood makes doomed attack on XX Corps and part of XXIII Corps at Kolb's Farm

10 27 June–2 July: XXIII Corps outflanks Confederate left and Johnston abandons his position

11 27 June: Sherman fails in an attempt to break through the Confederate centre at Kennesaw Mountain

12 5 July: Johnston establishes a new line on the north bank of the Chattahoochee

13 8–9 July: Federal XXIII Corps and cavalry cross the Chattahoochee. Johnston withdraws to Atlanta

into canals of sludge. The two armies danced in a close embrace towards Marietta, astride the railway, and Johnston entrenched along an immensely strong position on Kennesaw Mountain.

By this date Sherman's lines of communications stretched back almost 300 miles. Johnston ordered his brilliant but surly cavalry leader, Nathan Bedford Forrest, to strike the railways in central Tennessee and dislocate Sherman's logistics. Sherman's counter-measures ended in disaster with the Union defeat at Brice's Crossroads and he was forced to send reinforcements north which defeated Forrest (and wounded him) at Tupelo, Mississippi on 14 July. The depredations of Joseph

Wheeler against Sherman's vulnerable railway communications were reduced by providing a garrison along the line. But Sherman was alarmed at the defensive caste this gave to his strategy as well as the reduction it made to his front-line strength.

On 27 June, in a misguided attempt to maintain the pressure on Johnston, Sherman decided to assault the weakest part of the Kennesaw position, where a stream intersected Johnston's defences, on Pigeon Hill. Johnston's breastworks were very strong and the Union troops moved forward in temperatures of 100°F in the shade. They were exhausted before they went into the attack and Johnston's infantry repelled them effortlessly. Sherman lost 3,000 casualties to Johnston's 600. Yet Johnston could do nothing with this tactical victory, for Sherman retained the initiative and moved round his left, inching ever nearer Atlanta, whose spires could be seen clearly from the top of Kennesaw Mountain.

Johnston had no choice but to pull back once more and occupy a new defensive position (built by slaves) north of the Chattahoochee river. In exchanges with his anxious government, Johnston had claimed he could hold this position for two months, but Sherman had already begun to penetrate it by the time Johnston had occupied it fully on 3 July. Johnston was pushed back by his left a further twelve miles; and in a clever two-fisted manoeuvre, Sherman was completely across the Chattahoochee by 9 July. Johnston withdrew again to Peach Tree Creek only four miles away from the centre of Atlanta. This withdrawal triggered frantic discussions in Richmond. The President had received detailed written briefings from Hood and dispatched Braxton Bragg to explore the available courses of action and report back. Bragg believed that Johnston had played a part in his own dismissal the previous November, and was not of a forgiving disposition. Bragg consulted Hood who argued that the Army of Tennessee must attack. Davis hesitated and tried to give Johnston one more chance by telegraphing him for his plans. Always inflexible and unhelpful when dealing with his political masters (mainly because he was closely allied with a leading critic of the administration, Senator Louis T. Wigfall), Johnston refused to disclose them. It was wholly symptomatic of his military style that he said his plan 'must depend upon that of the enemy'. He also hinted that he would have to give up Atlanta. This was wholly unacceptable politically to Davis, as Atlanta had become a symbol of Confederate resistance. Johnston was relieved of command and replaced by the youthful and impulsive Hood.

Sherman was pleased by Hood's appointment. He knew that intellect and good sense were not among his most striking assets and that he would attack regardless. On 20 July Hood tried to take Thomas's Army of the Cumberland by surprise as it crossed Peach Tree Creek, but his assault was badly timed and disjointed, and the Confederates were thrown back. The following day Hood withdrew into the city's defences and then tried again. He sent his men on a wearying southerly march in the summer heat in an effort to strike McPherson's flank. McPherson was killed during this surprise attack, but it was badly organized and eventually driven back with heavy casualties. Indeed in this one afternoon Hood's troops suffered half as many casualties as the entire Army of Tennessee in Johnston's three months of active campaigning. Sherman gave McPherson's corps to Oliver O. Howard rather than to John A. Logan, by far the best of the so-called 'political generals', who greatly resented being passed over.

Sherman now realized, as Grant had been forced to besiege Richmond, that the Atlanta campaign was politically critical; indeed the very future of the Lincoln Administration rested upon it. Even the President himself doubted whether he would be re-elected. The Grant–Sherman team had expended 90,000 Union casualties for little gain, and pressure to end the war was growing. Sherman shifted from the right flank to his left and moved around the city to cut its last railway link. Hood tried to block this move at the battle of Ezra Church, but Sherman, with a phlegmatic dedication worthy of Grant, would not be deflected from his goal of strangling Atlanta into surrender. In one last desperate ploy, Hood sent two corps to attack the

Union lines at Jonesboro, twenty miles south of Atlanta. The Union troops were entrenched and Hood's attacks overstrained the capacity of his troops who were repulsed. Sherman then counter-attacked, and to avoid being trapped, as Pemberton had been in Vicksburg, Hood evacuated the city on 1 September 1864. Hood and Sherman became involved in an acrimonious correspondence concerning the latter's treatment of the civilian population, as they were eventually forced out of their homes and Atlanta was put to the torch. In a later famous exchange, Sherman told the protesting mayor, 'War is cruelty and you cannot refine it.' Sherman's action, combined with Sheridan's systematic campaign against the farms of the Shenandoah Valley, signalled that civilians could not be immune from the Union's overall attritional policy. Sherman would develop this aspect of his strategy in the next phase of his campaign.

Sherman was a brilliant writer and a no less striking phrase was used in his dispatch to Lincoln: 'Atlanta is ours and fairly won.' The fall of

The destruction of Confederate rolling stock at Atlanta in 1864. In addition to its symbolic significance, Atlanta was a vital communications centre and railroad junction. Its loss was a catastrophe for the Confederacy.

Atlanta was one of the most important military events of the war. It guaranteed Lincoln's re-election and thus the continuance of the strategy of unconditional and complete Confederate surrender. Accordingly, Sherman's victory transformed the political landscape and Lincoln was triumphantly re-elected the following November. Democratic party talk of an armistice with the Confederacy had now lost all credibility.

Sherman then applied his restless intelligence to his new plan of campaign. Hood's army had lost Atlanta but it had not been destroyed. As Sherman advanced south and east into the Confederate heartland he was faced with the problem of what to do with it. Holding his long lines of communication was costing him 1,000 men per month. Matters took a turn for the worse when Hood, completely disregarding logistical reality, slipped behind Sherman and began to move back towards Chattanooga. Briefly, Sherman followed him back the way he had just come, traversing in reverse the hotly contested battlefields of North Georgia. He persuaded Grant of the merits of a plan to march into Georgia. 'I could cut a swath through to the sea,' he informed the general-in-chief enthusiastically, 'divide the Confederacy in two, and come up on the rear of Lee.' Neither the President nor Grant was too keen on this plan at first. But when Sherman sent Thomas and the 62,000 men of the Army of the Cumberland to Nashville to deal with Hood, they were convinced of its merits and he was given permission to carry it out.

Sherman was able to advance into the very vitals of the Confederacy because Hood had, by his own volition, vacated the main theatre of operations. Hood's hope that Sherman would be forced to give up all that he had gained in the previous move on Atlanta proved empty. It was a curious state of affairs with opposing armies moving in opposite directions. In his *Memoirs* Sherman characterized his marches as a 'shift of base', a movement 'from the interior to a point on the sea-coast from which it could achieve other important results'. It was thus a means to an end 'and not an essential act of war'. Thus the later construction placed upon Sherman's marches by the military theorist

Captain B. H. Liddell Hart, namely, that they were important prototypes of the 'indirect approach', was somewhat exaggerated. None the less, these were important steps forward in the industrialization of war. Sherman's prime target was the enemy's war-making resources and his morale. Property rather than the people themselves was Sherman's target. He was also involved in a psychological war – for he aimed to attack the civil will as well as the morale of the enemy army. If he was fighting a hostile people as well as armies then they, too, should feel 'the hard hand of war'. Then the Southern people would appreciate the futility of continued resistance.

The march to Savannah on the Atlantic Coast – a distance of 285 miles – was undertaken on a broad front with four corps and a strong cavalry screen which moved to and fro, wherever the danger from Confederate cavalry was strongest. The army was stretched out over sixty miles, as it dispersed to subsist; but unlike Lee's efforts to gain

SHERMAN'S MARCHES

Sherman's main aim in his famous marches through Georgia and the Carolinas was the passage of his army through Confederate territory, and to inflict as much damage as he could on Southern war-making resources. He was impressed by his troops' desire for revenge on South Carolina. 'I almost tremble at her fate,' he told Halleck, 'but feel that she deserves all that seems to be in store for her.'

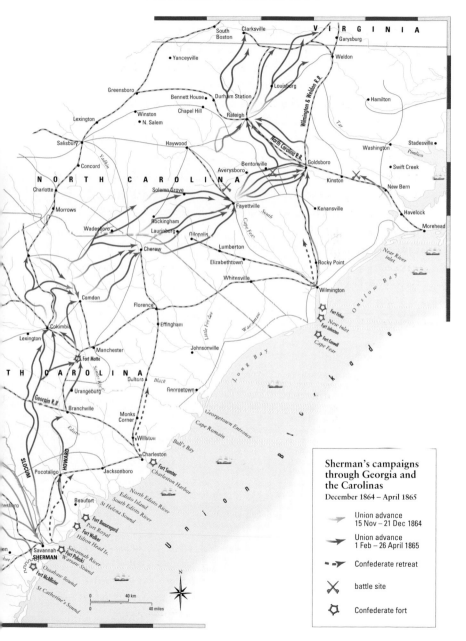

Sherman's campaigns through Georgia and the Carolinas

December 1864 – April 1865

Union advance
15 Nov – 21 Dec 1864

Union advance
1 Feb – 26 April 1865

Confederate retreat

battle site

Confederate fort

similar logistic nourishment in 1862, Sherman's troops were in little danger because of Hood's advance into Tennessee. They were given orders 'to forage liberally on the country', but Sherman recognized the fine line between destroying the enemy's resources and rampant vandalism, because an orgy of the latter would rot the fabric of discipline of his army. Passions were stoked by the arrival of the first prisoners from the prison camp at Andersonville. Their emaciated state did much to confirm the worst stereotypes of anti-Southern propaganda – that Southerners were brutal, selfish savages. Passions of war in the industrial age, as in any other, are not always amenable to reason. The next stage of the campaign embraced an advance northwards into South Carolina. A desire for revenge does much to explain the behaviour of Sherman's veterans in South Carolina, who were determined to punish this hotbed of secession for starting the war. But the extent of their brutality was exaggerated by post-1865 Southern apologists, especially when compared to, say, Second World War atrocities; most violence was to buildings rather than women and children; and the infamous

The destruction of Charleston, South Carolina in 1865. Union troops looked foward to advancing on South Carolina, the nest of secessionist sentiment. 'We will let her know,' an Ohio private boasted, 'that it isn't so sweet to secede as she thought it would be.'

burnings of non-military targets, such as the burning of Columbia, South Carolina in February 1865, were started more by accident than design. By the end of March, with astonishing speed and tenacity of purpose, Sherman's veterans had crossed the state line into North Carolina and borne down on Virginia. His rear had been secured by Thomas's stunning victory at Nashville in December 1864 which had, to all intents and purposes, destroyed the Army of Tennessee and Hood's feckless scheme of advancing to the Ohio river.

In February 1865 Lee was somewhat belatedly appointed general-in-chief of the Confederacy. He still commanded the Army of Northern Virginia as well, but the effective strength of the Confederacy had so shrunk after Sherman's Marches that his army was its last effective military force. One of Lee's first acts was to appoint Joseph E. Johnston as the commander of what remained of Confederate military forces in North Carolina. Johnston successfully caught Sherman wrong-footed at the battle of Bentonville in March 1865, but his forces were simply too weak to secure decisive results. As neighbouring Union corps advanced on Johnston's force, he withdrew hurriedly from the field.

Lee's predicament was equally hopeless. During the previous months Grant had edged westwards in an attempt to stretch Lee's lines to breaking point and then decisively cut Richmond's railway communications westwards. Once Petersburg had fallen the capital of the Confederacy would be untenable. Lee attempted to arrest this process by his desperate assault at Fort Stedman on the night of 24/25 March, but the Army of Northern Virginia was repulsed. Even the spirit of those troops most suited to a rapid war of manoeuvre is eroded by prolonged exposure to static warfare, and Lee's predictions of the dire consequences for his troops of a siege were more than fulfilled. On 29 March Sheridan's troops from the Shenandoah Valley returned to take their place in Grant's line. Grant ordered Sheridan to envelop Lee's right at Five Forks. Moving more rapidly and decisively than his Confederate counterpart, George E. Pickett, Sheridan won an important success. The battle of Five Forks was the first outright

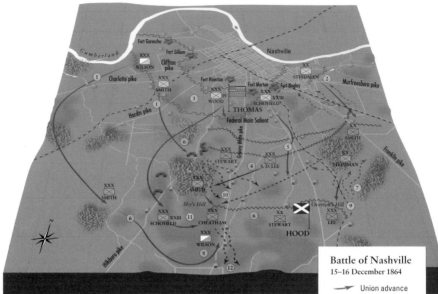

NASHVILLE

*Thomas's Army of the Cumberland protected Sherman's rear.
Thomas effected a concentration at Nashville, while Scholfield
inflicted a severe repulse on Hood's reckless assaults at Franklin.
In December 1864 he launched a powerful attack on Hood's
ragged columns, shattering his right with savage blows on two
successive days.*

Battle of Nashville
15–16 December 1864

→ Union advance

→ Confederate advance

⇢ Union retreat

⇢ Confederate retreat

🛡 fort

⬛ redoubt

(1) 15 December, *c.* 10 am: Wilson's cavalry corps and A. J. Smith's infantry corps begin to swing round to attack Confederate left

(2) *c.* 11 am: Steedman's Provisional Detachment attacks Confederate right in a diversion and is repulsed

(3) *c.* 1 pm: Schofield's XXIII Corps advances to support Wilson's and Smith's attack

(4) *c.* 1 pm: Hood sends Johnson's division of Lee's corps to reinforce his left

(5) *c.* 2 pm: Kimball's and Beatty's divisions of Wood's IV Corps assail Confederate centre

(6) Late pm: Wilson's and Smith's attack drives Confederates from Hillsboro Pike. Hood withdraws to line covering the Granny White and Franklin pikes

(7) 16 December, *c.* 10 am: Steedman attacks Confederate right on Overton Hill, and is repulsed

(8) 12 noon: Wilson reaches rear of Confederate left

(9) *c.* 3.30 pm: Beatty and Steedman make another unsuccessful Federal attack on Overton's Hill

(10) 4 pm: Elements of Smith's corps break Confederate line at Shy's Hill

(11) *c.* 4.30 pm: Wilson attacks Confederate left from south, Schofield from west, and Smith from north, routing Cheatham's and Stewart's corps

(12) Evening and night: Remnants of Cheatham's and Smith's corps flee south along Granny White pike

Matthew Brady's last photograph of Lincoln, taken in April 1865. Lincoln had persevered, but in the memorable words of the historian Richard Hofstadter, 'He had had his ambitions and fulfilled them, and met heartache in his triumph.'

offensive victory won by the Army of the Potomac over its Confederate rival. It was perhaps the most timely. Grant ordered an assault on Petersburg, which fell. On 1 April 1865 Lee wrote to President Davis informing him that he was evacuating the city, a letter that was handed to Davis while he was attending church that Sunday. Once the Army of Northern Virginia had evacuated its trenches it was vulnerable to the overwhelming forces that Grant directed masterfully, intent on its destruction. Organizing a brilliant double envelopment, Grant cut Lee's army in two at Sayler's Creek, and then trapped him by sending Sheridan's cavalry ahead of the infantry, to pin the Confederates in place before the infantry arrived. On 9 April, almost exactly four years after the war had broken out, Lee was forced to surrender the Army of Northern Virginia at Appomattox Court House. Lee's attempt to negotiate a general surrender was rejected, leaving no hope for the Confederates but acquiescence in a further series of piecemeal surrenders. After Lee's, the most important was the capitulation, on 26 April, of Johnston to Sherman at Durham Station, North Carolina, which followed the assassination of Abraham Lincoln.

The significance of this war will be reviewed at the end of the book. It had cost 620,000 American soldiers' lives, 360,000 Union and 260,000 Confederate. The numbers of civilians killed cannot be estimated accurately. Certainly these military casualties, especially in the South, represent greater percentage losses than those Britain was to endure in the First World War. As for the devastation inflicted on the South, this was enormous. The Southern economy was totally ruined and that damage was to linger for over a century, not to recover fully until our own day in the guise of the 'Sun Belt'. In 1861–5 the total capital of the South, agricultural and industrial, shrank by 46 per cent. Northern capital, by contrast, grew by 50 per cent. In 1860 the slave states contained 30 per cent of the total wealth of the United States; by 1870 this figure had fallen to a mere 12 per cent. There can be no doubting the war's political significance either. Secession as a political issue was ended once and for all. Slavery was destroyed and the power of the federal government greatly augmented. Now conscious of that great power, Grant and others pressed for a conclusion to French military intervention in the affairs of Mexico, and by 1868 Napoleon III had brought this ill-fated adventure to an end. His determined attempts to seek compensation for his embarrassment over Mexico would have baleful consequences for the future history of Europe.

Ruined Richmond after its surrender in April 1865. Following Lee's evacuation, chaos and riots ensued. The hungry broke into the government commissary to find food and prevented the Virginia militia from pouring barrels of liquor into the streets. Fire was ignited after shells exploded from the burning armoury. Its effects have been captured beautifully by Brady. The Virginia State capitol (seat of the Confederate Congress) broods over a desolate scene.

CHAPTER FIVE

The German Wars of Unification 1864, 1866, 1870–71

The growing industrial power of Prussia, linked with the army reforms of Moltke and Roon, provided the means 'iron and blood' In Bismarck's famous formulation – by which he unified Germany and made it the greatest power in Europe. It also indicated that in future wars the mobilization of a nation's entire industrial capacity was the secret of victory over other major powers. Such a mobilization required a strict policing of the home front. In October 1870 royal headquarters issued instructions to 'immediately report anyone who by public statement supported France in its resistance to German conditions for peace ... These persons are to be arrested as long as the state of siege [i.e. war] is in effect.'

The German Wars of Unification

THE ROLE OF OUTSIDE powers was crucial in determining the character of the German Wars of Unification. During the American Civil War, the failure of Britain and France to intervene allowed the North to build up its military strength and smash the South; moreover, it remained a civil war. The three Prussian wars remained short in duration and limited in character – mainly because Prussian military preparation was sufficient to win an outright victory in the first phase. In 1864 Prussia and Austria co-operated to take the duchies of Schleswig and Holstein from Denmark. The main significance of this war was to demonstrate the superiority of the Prussian breech-loading rifle, the 'needle gun', which made short work of brave but hopelessly out-classed Danish infantry. Prussia was intent on dominating the thirty-nine states of the Deutscher Bund, or Rhine Confederation, for it produced 80 per cent of Germany's coal and steel. French policy was to maintain this area in a state of permanent division, and at Olmütz in 1850 Prussia acknowledged Austrian supremacy within the Confederation. After 1852, when Otto von Bismarck became Chancellor, his policy revolved around the dismantling of the Olmütz agreement, the removal of French and Austrian influence and the domination of Germany by Prussia. In the series of wars that he launched, the place of national aspirations and unification – as again with the American case – was vital.

Bismarck had signed an alliance with Italy to create a southern front against Austria. When the Austrians raised the question of the

THE EXPANSION OF PRUSSIA
As to the complexities of the Schleswig-Holstein issue, the British prime minister, Lord Palmerston, declared that only three people had ever understood it: the Prince Consort, Albert, who had died; a professor, who had been driven insane by it; and himself, who had forgotten all he knew.

Expansion of Prussia
1815–71

Prussia in 1815

border of German Confederation, 1815

Prussian gains by 1867

border of North German Confederation, 1867

German states joining the Confederation in 1871 including Alsace and Lorraine taken from France

border of German Empire, 1871

German Confederation

Prussia

battle, with date

1. Grand Duchy of Oldenburg
2. Mecklenburg-Strelitz
3. Schaumburg-Lippe
4. Lippe-Detmold
5. Duchy of Brunswick
6. Duchy of Anhalt
7. Thuringian States
8. Waldeck
9. Lichtenberg
10. Principality of Hohenzollern
11. Grand Duchy of Luxemburg

NORWAY
not independent until 1905

KINGDOM OF SWEDEN

KINGDOM OF DENMARK

North Sea

Baltic Sea

Schleswig
Kiel
Holstein
Lübeck
Rostock
Hamburg
Gr. Duchy of Mecklenburg-Schwerin
Bremen
Stettin
Königsberg
Danzig
East Prussia
West Prussia
Bromberg
Pomerania

NETHERLANDS

Hanover
Berlin
Magdeburg
Brandenburg
Posen
Posen
Warsaw

BELGIUM
Westphalia
Düsseldorf
Cologne
Bonn
Hesse
Koblenz
Frankfurt
Gr. Duchy

1839 to Belgium

RUSSIAN
Lodz
Poland
EMPIRE
Breslau
Silesia
Leipzig
Dresden
K. OF SAXONY
Erfurt

1870 Sedan
Lorraine
Mannheim
Alsace
Grand Duchy of Baden
Bâle
Neuchâtel 1815–57 to Prussia

FRANCE

Prague
Bohemia
1866 Königgrätz (Sadowa)
Olmütz
Moravia

Republic of Cracow 1846 to Austria

Nuremberg
KINGDOM OF WÜRTTEMBERG
KINGDOM OF BAVARIA
Munich
Danube

AUSTRO-HUNGARIAN EMPIRE
Linz
Vienna
Bratislava
Salzburg
Danube
Budapest

Zürich
SWITZERLAND
Tyrol
Austria
Graz
Hungary

ITALY

administration of Schleswig and Holstein in the Confederation's Diet, they gave Bismarck a pretext for declaring war in 1866 and occupying the two duchies. Italy wanted to 'redeem' the entire Italian peninsula from Austrian rule by occupying Venetia. No great power shared the Austrian view that German and Italian unification posed a threat to the balance of power. Austria was forced to fight Prussia and Italy on her own.

A good Austrian general could have exploited Prussia's weaknesses. Of all considerable European powers, Prussia was the most vulnerable to invasion. Her territories were straddled across central Europe and poorly consolidated; the telegraph and railway accentuated this weakness. The Austrians had revealed their own significant deficiencies during the Franco-Austrian War of 1859 where, at the battles of Montebello, Palestro and Magenta, great opportunities were missed. The power that learned the lessons of 1859 would win in 1866, lessons residing mainly in the strategic understanding that whichever power used the railways to launch the best organized and most powerful initial offensive would win the war. This Prussia was able to do, though the margin of superiority was not as great as contemporaries imagined. If Austria had taken advantage of its central position and interior lines by the use of railways, it could have divided the field forces between north and south, and then transported overwhelming strength to the threatened point. To succeed, decisive action was required – as Lee had furnished in Virginia in 1862. Yet Austrian forces dawdled and they failed to act with dispatch.

This was hardly surprising, because the Austrian commanders were poor. The Austrian Chief of Staff, General Alfred Henikstein, was an over-promoted lightweight, with trifling qualifications for the post and slight experience. He was over-borne by the mountainous Austrian bureaucracy, but was at least a friend of the field commander, the *Feldzugmeister*, Ludwig Benedek. Benedek had an inflated reputation as a result of the courage he had shown at Solferino. He was a flamboyant personality of strong opinions, rather like Joseph Hooker, and like Hooker he was happiest at corps level. Unlike Hooker he lacked ideas and relied totally on his pedantic chief of staff, Gideon Krismanic. Benedek was ill-equipped for fighting a war at the operational level. He boasted that he had not read a book since he had graduated from war college many years before. Benedek was of the opinion that the only talents needed for high command 'are a strong stomach and a good digestion'. As for the staff he assembled to help him, they were purely decorative and in aggregate made for an entertaining dining club. Benedek had no time for a proper staff system whose members he dismissed as 'blue-blooded baboons'.

He was confronted by Helmuth von Moltke, a soldier of an entirely different order. Moltke still had not imposed his absolute authority over the Prussian military system: 'Who is this fellow, von Moltke?' a subordinate asked during the 1866 campaign. By its conclusion the question would not need to be asked again. Moltke's system rested on dynamism in the offensive, using the railway to improve the Napoleonic formula of 'march divided, fight united'. Envelopment was the key to victory because, Moltke realized, 'an army hit in front and flank finds that its *strategic* advantage of internal lines [has] been beaten *tactically*'. The commander who gained the initial advantage seized the initiative and imposed his plan on the enemy. To that end Moltke used all five railway lines available to him in his movement south. He intended to transport 200,000 men to the decisive point. American observers were astonished to discover that Moltke made little preparation for their supply, and concluded (quite rightly) that, logistically, American staffs were superior. However, American generals, especially McClellan, were inclined to fuss too much over lines of supply to the detriment of operations, and this was an error that Moltke never made. The Austrian Army was superior in terms of numbers, deploying ten corps of 400,000 to Prussia's eight corps of 300,000; but Benedek was forced to detach forces to the Italian front, leaving seven corps of 245,000 plus six cavalry divisions for the important northern front. By intelligent use of the railway during mobilization, Moltke was able to achieve local superiority with

*Emperor Franz Joseph promoted Benedek in a
political ploy. He hoped to exploit Benedek's
handsome appearance and reputation for courage
among Austria's newly enfranchised middle
class. The decision was disastrous. The Emperor
was forced to intervene in the face of Benedek's
procrastination when the Prussians invaded
in 1866.*

254,000 men. Yet the Prussians committed
some serious errors. The railway lines were
clogged, 18,000 tons of supplies were
allowed to rot in neglected branch lines
and once the Prussian armies crossed the
Austrian frontier the railway system had no
impact on the military operations at all.

Moltke divided his forces into four. The
smallest columns dealt with the German
states: Hanover, Baden-Württemberg and Bavaria. The largest were
concentrated in three field armies: the Elbe, the First and the Second
Armies. The Elbe Army was to secure the Prussian right flank, occupy
Saxony and take Dresden, then align itself with First Army. The First
and Second Armies were to invade Bohemia, locate Benedek's Army
and destroy it in the vicinity of Königgrätz; the Elbe and First Armies
were to fix it in a defensive position, the Second Army was to envelop
it, smashing its right flank. Benedek had received complete details of
Moltke's plan from Austrian agents but he did nothing. Benedek's fatal
indecision was the most important factor working in Moltke's favour.
Not knowing what to do, he dithered or sought refuge in detail and the
trivial. He developed a routine at headquarters that involved much
nugatory activity but no thought – let alone attention to the pressing
matters that really counted, such as formulating an operational plan.
Like McClellan, he inspected troops and organized luncheons; but
unlike the 'Young Napoleon' he had no elevated thoughts. He went out

for long walks and in the evening visited the local *gasthaus* for a libation. This inactivity allowed Moltke to pick off Austria's German allies one by one (even though they dismantled their railways in a desperate effort to slow down the Prussian advance), and then occupy Dresden. The Prussian First and Second Armies began their advance on 23 and 26 June 1866 and succeeded in occupying northern Bohemia, in a virtually unopposed advance. In frustration,Emperor Franz Joseph ordered Benedek to do something and advance towards Josephstadt. But the confusion caused by this preremptory order only provided Moltke with another ten days in which to complete his concentration unmolested. Yet there was still a chance that, if Benedek moved swiftly, he could block the Prussian advance through the Giant Mountains and destroy each army as it debouched through the passes.

The third week of June opened well for Austria with the news of a victory over Italy at Custozza. The Italian generals had never really worked out a concept of operations for their campaign; their direction was confused and the courage of individual Italian soldiers was no compensation for their incompetence. Had Benedek summoned reinforcements from the Italian front at once, he could have guaranteed numerical superiority for his offensive against the Prussians. But Benedek did nothing. His lines of communication consisted of one railway track back to Vienna, but it was his personal failings rather than any organizational weaknesses which permitted the waste of opportunities. Some observers gained solace from his silence; it was rumoured that his plan, not yet disclosed, was of such surpassing brilliance that he could only share it with his immediate staff; the staff wondered what it could be.

Eventually Benedek decided that he would attack the Elbe and First Armies with his North Army and then turn on Moltke's Second Army. Moltke welcomed news of Benedek's advance, because he believed that by advancing north and west Benedek was putting his head into the noose that would be tightened by the Second Army. Second Army's progress through the Giant Mountains was not impeded, even though

the Prussian columns were 50 kms long and it took four hours to
traverse the length of the column. Having been given a chance to set
their plan in motion the Prussians were always able to gain their
objectives just before the Austrians moved to frustrate them. The liberty
of manoeuvre thus achieved tended to set any tactical victories gained
by the Austrians, such as Trautenau on 27 June, at nought because the
Austrian victors were invariably outflanked by the other advancing
armies and forced to retreat. These days were nevertheless frustrating
for Moltke because his cables from Berlin were taking more than twelve
hours to reach his subordinates' headquarters. Then he learnt that
Prince Frederick Charles, commanding First Army, was defying his plan
by diverging westwards in the pursuit of a tactical success that would
redound to his glory but endanger the entire concept of operations.
Moltke decided to move to Bohemia himself so that he could control

Success for Steinmetz's V Corps at Skalice over the Austrian VI and VIII Corps.
Steinmetz, not over-endowed with brains or imagination, gazes over the scene of his
triumph. Moltke had difficulty in reining in such commanders because their pursuit
of local objectives threatened to overturn his operational design.

his armies more tightly. The temporary breakdown of Moltke's plan presented Benedek with another golden opportunity to move with overwhelming strength to annihilate Second Army; but this opportunity, like all the others, was passed up.

Benedek decided eventually to advance on the Jicin plateau to secure a central position from which he could defeat the Prussian armies separately. This was a good idea, but the move should have been made two weeks before. In three successive engagements the Crown Prince ordered the Second Army to attack at Burkersdorf, Rudersdorf and Skalice on 29 June. All three of these engagements demonstrated the superiority of the Prussian needle-gun over the massed, frontal charges of the Austrian infantry. Later that day Jicin itself fell and thus dislocated Benedek's plan. Moltke could henceforth concentrate as he chose without interference from the Austrians. Benedek, close to nervous collapse, withdrew to a position at Königgrätz which, though tactically strong, led to the overcrowding of his army of almost a quarter of a million on a ridge less than 8 kilometres long; operationally, he was allowing himself to be enveloped and annihilated by three armies. Yet he occupied his mind with the layout of his camp, overwhelmed by the weight of his responsibilities. The only factor that might impede the realization of Moltke's plan was logistic – the soldiers of First Army were starving hungry; something that would never have happened in the Army of the Potomac.

None the less Moltke showed an energy and flexibility alien to McClellan by altering his plan on the night of 2 July. Fearful that Benedek would withdraw to the east bank of the Elbe and establish a formidable, entrenched position, he ordered Second Army to attack immediately the following day and smash into Benedek's right at Chlum. Prince Frederick Charles was to fix Benedek on the Sadowa–Nechanitz front while the Army of the Elbe guarded the right flank. But the following morning the ardent Frederick Charles was not one to play second fiddle and transformed this holding operation into a decisive, frontal assault on Benedek's line. Fortunately, his error was

Austro-Prussian War 1866

- Prussian territory
- Italy, allied to Prussia
- allied or sympathetic to Prussia
- Austrian territory
- allied or sympathetic to Austria
- neutral States
- major railways
- Prussian campaigns
- Austrian attacks
- Italian attacks
- territory gained by Italy after hostilities
- battle

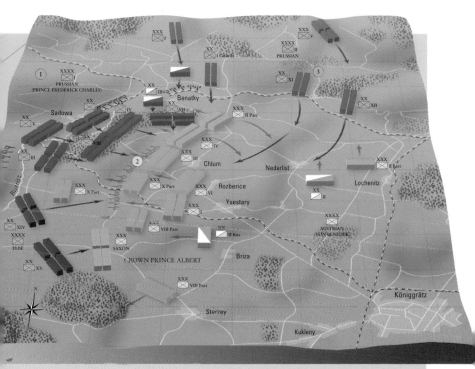

KÖNNIGRÄTZ

This campaign is a text-book example of Moltke's dictum, 'march divided, fight united'. Moltke had very good luck throughout the campaign, and profited from Benedek's inability to concentrate his troops to impede the Prussian junction on ground of Moltke's choosing.

1 Dawn: the Prussian First and Elbe Armies launch their attack; meanwhile the Prussian Second Army fails to move, by error having not received the order to attack

2 Austrian counter-attacks and artillery hold the Prussian attacks, but Von Benedek fails to use his cavalry. The Austrians lose the advantage as the Prussians bring up reserve artillery

3 Eventually a courier reaches the Prussian Second Army with orders to attack. By 2.30 pm this is under way and the Austrians begin to withdraw, covered by artillery

redressed by the failure of the Austrian IV Corps to secure Chlum, as it preferred to advance westwards. Just as Prince Frederick Charles warned that he might have to withdraw, Second Army saved the day by appearing on the battlefield at about 2 p.m. Benedek personally directed small unit tactics but he fundamentally mismanaged the battle. An Austrian counter-attack towards Chlum was driven back and their line of retreat was endangered. Massed Austrian cavalry charges, in particular, paid an extremely high price.

Benedek had no alternative but to withdraw. As the Prussian Army was too confused by its concentration on the ground (rather than in the environs of the battlefield, as Moltke had planned originally), there was no pursuit. On 26 July Austria sued for peace. Benedek had lost almost 30 per cent of the force that he had originally mustered. In eight days he had sustained 10,000 killed, 27,800 wounded and 43,200 prisoners. The

The Prussians, firing their needle-guns, defend the Svib Wood near Cistoves, as the Austrians try and envelop the Prussian First Army before the Second arrives. So devastating were the casualties inflicted on the Austrians that the Hungarians held back. 'Their officers could not budge them,' it was reported.

A man with a huge appetite for power – with an appetite for food to match. Bismarck would consume a huge supper before retiring. He then lay sleepless because of indigestion, brooding on past slights. He declared one morning, 'I have spent the whole night hating.'

Prussians had lost 9,500 at Könnigrätz, a fraction of Benedek's losses. During the negotiations leading to the armistice Bismarck made no territorial claims on Austria, but he demanded an indemnity of 30 million florins to pay for the war, and an acknowledgement from Franz Joseph that Austria would withdraw from German affairs. Prussia's staff system had won a stunning success, but Moltke had enjoyed good luck. He had also learnt an important lesson that had eluded McClellan and Hooker, despite the able schemes that they had produced, namely, that no plan survives first contact with the enemy.

Moltke was to develop the techniques that he pioneered in 1866 further in the Franco-Prussian War of 1870 71. Like the American Civil War, the Franco-Prussian War was triggered by the side standing on the defensive, France. The war was actually provoked by Bismarck. France, after the ill-fated Mexican adventure, needed a foreign policy success to bolster the declining prestige of the Second Empire. The actual spark that set the conflict aflame was the Hohenzollern candidature for the Spanish throne, vacant since the revolution of 1868. With Bismarck's support, it was offered to Prince Leopold of Hohenzollern-Sigmaringen; but France claimed that such an offer was an insult. After Bismarck had doctored the telegram from the King of Prussia's holiday resort at Ems indicating intransigence, France declared war. Napoleon III believed that he could win a quick victory. As Michael Howard sums up: by a 'tragic combination of ill-luck, stupidity and ignorance, France blundered into war'. Moreover, outside powers remained neutral. It would be a straight duel between France and Prussia.

French confidence was bolstered by their reliance on an army of long-service veterans who had performed well in Mexico and North Africa. The Prussian force of conscripts was dismissed as an army of 'lawyers and oculists'. Moltke feared that the French railway system was better than the Prussian, and would help the French defence. However, French mobilization was chaotic in the extreme, with troops stationed near the Prussian border being called up via their home bases in Algiers. One French general telegraphed Paris, 'Have arrived at Belfort. Not found my brigade. Not found general division. What should I do? Don't know where my regiments are.' Such levels of confusion helped Moltke, and he was able to complete his mobilization and advance into French territory unmolested. This kind of situation underlines the importance of the railway in nineteenth-century warfare. As in the American Civil War in 1861–5, the experience of the Prussian wars of 1866 and 1870–71 demonstrates that its main value was in mobilizing military force and bringing it to the battlefield; its power was essentially strategic and logistic. It could aid strategic envelopment, but with the enhanced power of the rifle and artillery it could not aid tactical envelopment on the battlefield. Indeed, once the armies had moved beyond their railheads campaigns were fought, with men marching across the battlefield in the traditional way, rather like those of the Napoleonic wars. But in 1870 neither side made much use of entrenchments, and troops still stood out in the open.

If the war had continued much beyond the opening battles on the frontiers, doubtless that condition would have changed. Some later critics put this Napoleonic, perverse refusal to entrench down to an ignorance or condescension towards the American Civil War. Moltke was reported to have said that the Civil War consisted of 'two armed mobs chasing another' around the countryside 'from which nothing can be learned'. Both General Sherman and General Sheridan were to visit the Prussian armies at various times. In 1872 Sherman visited Moltke and was asked to confirm that Moltke had indeed made such a sweeping statement. He replied sharply: 'I did not ask him the question because I did not presume that he was such an ass as to say that.' The attribution is certainly apocryphal. That the Franco-Prussian War did not become entrenched is simply due to the fact that Moltke again had the good fortune to win his victories in the first phase. Had the French generals capitalized on their tactical successes and Moltke been frustrated, then the tactical defence would have gained in strength as the conflict became more attritional.

As in 1866, Moltke enjoyed a key advantage provided by the low calibre of his enemies. Napoleon III was ailing; he strove to interfere yet abdicated the responsibility to his marshals. In any case, the French lacked a general staff or any system of higher command training. Moltke also enjoyed a numerical superiority. The Prussian system of conscription presented him with an army of 484,000 men and 50,000 horses. The French Army was 343,000 strong, although many were veterans. Moltke organized three armies: First Army (Steinmetz), Second Army (Prince Frederick Charles) and Third Army (Crown Prince); in all, he had fourteen corps to deploy for the invasion of France, of about 29,000 men each. All the non Prussian corps received the same allocation of general staff officers as the Prussian corps, three at corps and one each at division; these officers were Moltke's representatives and owed their prime allegiance to him and not to their respective commanders. The Prussian mobilization was far from perfect, though superior to the French. Trains were up to two days late and not enough attention had been devoted to administering movement forward from the railheads; delays in consolidating the corps were experienced. Logistics were also neglected: 16,830 tons of supplies were lost in the lines of communication.

Moltke's plan was to advance into France with the First and Second Armies fixing the French in the Saarland. Once the flank of Second Army was secure, Prince Frederick Charles was to move behind the

Courageous and zealous, Marshal MacMahon appealed to Bazaine, his superior, for orders. 'I presume that the minister will have given you orders,' Bazaine replied mystifyingly, 'your operations being at the moment entirely outside my zone of action.'

flank of the French Army in Lorraine and smash it against the Saar. In the meantime Third Army was to destroy French resistance in Alsace. The whole scheme was an envelopment on a grand scale. But, as Moltke might have expected, once the invasion began things did not go according to plan. Third Army was delayed; First Army disobeyed orders and moved south-east across routes allotted to Second Army; and as the cavalry had been placed at the back of each infantry corps, the Prussians groped forward blindly.

The first battles came in Alsace. The French commander in the region, Marshal MacMahon, was very typical of the Napoleonic generals of this generation. He was brave, much liked by the soldiers, a stout tactician, but was lacking in imagination and operational insight. Also the telegraph had not helped him because ease of communication had prompted misleading information and wasted movement in the summer heat. In two battles fought on 6 August 1870 at Wörth and Spicheren, the French chassepot proved superior to the Prussian needle-gun. Yet the French were forced to withdraw despite their defensive successes by Prussian enveloping tactics. At Spicheren, Marshal Bazaine showed a lack of grip on the battle that augured badly for the future. These two actions allowed a Prussian penetration of the French frontier positions, the result of which was curious. The French withdrew westwards, but as the enveloping Prussian columns turned to annihilate

Marshal Bazaine had risen from the ranks and would not win any beauty contests. The courtiers among his brother marshals seemed to sense that he was the ideal scapegoat should things go wrong. Half-hearted and hesitant, he was later accused of treachery.

their adversaries, they moved eastwards, so that both sides were moving in the opposite directions to those they were expected to take, given the French defence and the Prussian offence.

Napoleon III then decided to give up the supreme command. The senior commander was Marshal Canrobert, who had commanded in the Crimea. He declined the position and it devolved on Marshal Bazaine, a native of Alsace and an experienced colonial soldier; but he had never previously commanded more than 10,000 men in action. In character he resembled MacMahon, being courageous and at home with corps level tactics. Temperamentally he was unsuited to command at the highest levels. He lacked operational inspiration, was at a loss as to what action to take, and sought refuge in demanding trivia – like Benedek. At his court martial he admitted that 'command of 150,000 men is very difficult when one is unused to it'. Bazaine made no effective use of his chief of staff, General Jauras, whom he dismissed as the 'archivist'. During his first great battle, Bazaine set him to work out future promotions by dint of seniority. The demands of industrialized warfare would require a quite different character to wage it than an honest, courageous but bewildered fumbler like Bazaine.

The two French armies in Alsace and Lorraine had moved away from one another and Moltke strove to secure the line of the Moselle. He was advancing on a front of some forty miles. First Army was to fix the French to their positions while the Second drove into their flank. When Prince Frederick Charles seized the bridges over the Moselle and then began to move on the Meuse, it was clear that the French must withdraw, but five days were wasted before the orders were issued. On 15–16 August, as the First and Second Armies bore down from the west on the Metz–Verdun Road, Moltke was under the impression that he was approaching the rearguard of the Army of the Rhine, not its concentrated main body. He thus offered Bazaine an opportunity to

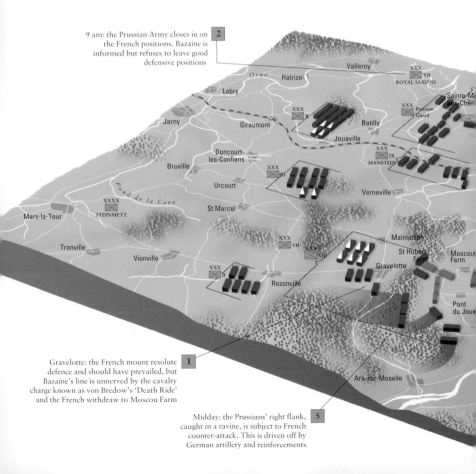

9 am: the Prussian Army closes in on the French positions. Bazaine is informed but refuses to leave good defensive positions **2**

Gravelotte: the French mount resolute defence and should have prevailed, but Bazaine's line is unnerved by the cavalry charge known as von Bredow's 'Death Ride' and the French withdraw to Moscou Farm **1**

Midday: the Prussians' right flank, caught in a ravine, is subject to French counter-attack. This is driven off by German artillery and reinforcements **5**

smash the Prussians piece by piece, and trap them in the French hinterland, separated from their lines of communications. Bazaine instead fought a series of actions between Gravelotte and St Privat, in which he very effectively snatched defeat from the jaws of victory. Bazaine, like Pemberton at Vicksburg in 1863, lacked confidence, and

GRAVELOTTE—ST PRIVAT

The Prussians are veering back towards the Moselle, while the French are facing westwards. But the Prussian envelopment has led to a momentary French advantage, as the French Army is concentrated while the Prussians are unprepared for battle. However, Bazaine throws away his opportunity. The repulse of the Prussian Guard at St Privat is not exploited. Eventually the Prussians work around Bazaine's right and take the village of St Privat. Bazaine then withdraws back into Metz.

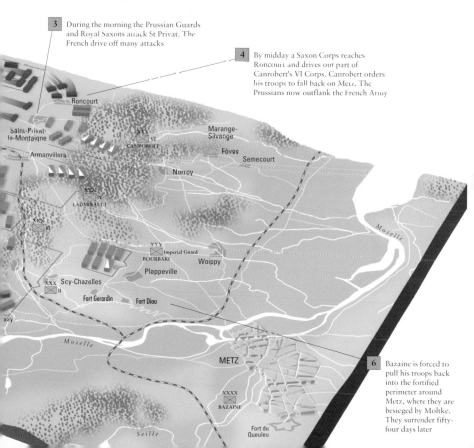

3 During the morning the Prussian Guards and Royal Saxons attack St Privat. The French drive off many attacks

4 By midday a Saxon Corps reaches Roncourt and drives out part of Canrobert's VI Corps. Canrobert orders his troops to fall back on Metz. The Prussians now outflank the French Army

6 Bazaine is forced to pull his troops back into the fortified perimeter around Metz, where they are besieged by Moltke. They surrender fifty-four days later

found the prospect of the defences of the fortress city of Metz very comforting. He devoted too much attention to ensuring a withdrawal into the city rather than launching an effective offensive that would win the campaign; deferring a decision was much more to his liking.

While Bazaine busied himself siting individual guns, Alvensleben's III Corps was repulsed by Canrobert's troops, but he, in turn, was confused by the psychological effect of a cavalry charge – von Bredow's 'Death Ride' – over dead ground into his flank. Bazaine was not available to take the decision and Canrobert withdrew. During the Prussian forward movement Steinmetz exceeded his orders and lost 6,000 men in a French rearguard action in the Mance ravine. Stupidity was by no means a French monopoly, and Steinmetz despised Moltke as a professorial pen-pusher; he was dismissed.

On 18 August, with 300,000 men crowded on to the battlefield, Moltke attempted to flank Bazaine out of his position by turning the French right and seizing the village of St Privat. The Prussian Guard Corps launched a frontal attack over open ground – rather like Grant's at Cold Harbor – and lost 8,000 men. Bazaine was not present on the field and claimed later that he had not heard the firing. The French Imperial Guard came up after the repulse of their Prussian counterpart, but nobody was effectively directing the battle. The commander of the Imperial Guard, General Bourbaki, became confused and thought that the French Army was withdrawing; he, too, ordered a withdrawal. The chance to smash Moltke's left flank was missed. During these actions the French lost 13,000 casualties but had inflicted 20,584 on the Prussians. They were the moral victors, but Bazaine could not turn a series of miscellaneous tactical successes into a coherent operational triumph. He withdrew into the fortress of Metz and offered Moltke an undeserved opportunity to win the campaign.

Moltke wrote a brilliant, short memorandum which he issued to his commanders that evening through his staff officers. It reorientated the point of main effort of the advance to the north now that Metz was masked. Moltke next ordered the creation of the Army of the Meuse;

the latter and Third Army were to close on the line of the River Meuse. If MacMahon withdrew to Paris with the Army of Châlons, then these two forces were to intercept him; if he moved south to relieve Bazaine, they were to smash his right; if he stayed where he was, then his army was to be enveloped and besieged in Sedan. Moltke's central, echeloned position and offensive outlook gave him the initiative and he moved to exploit it ruthlessly, not wasting a minute. His grasp of what was important in the higher level of the conduct of war is reminiscent of Ulysses S. Grant. Both Moltke and Grant were inferior to Lee as field commanders when it came to the sheer technique of commanding an army. But both had extensive experience of the highest command denied Lee until 1865, and thus should be judged the most consistently successful commanders of the age inaugurated by the Industrial Revolution. Moltke and Grant had much in common. Each was reserved and rather silent, detached and phlegmatic; each always remained calm and in control of his thoughts. Neither ever let his imagination run away with him. Both of them were fundamentally men of decision, for neither ever attempted to avoid harsh decisions when they were needed, and they both placed themselves at the most convenient location where they could direct operations. Moltke was the more aloof of the two, and Grant the more approachable. There was something indefinable about the two generals, but in the main, Grant was simultaneously more matter-of-fact and enigmatic than Moltke: a mystery to his contemporaries, who tended to underrate him.

Moltke was more overtly intellectual, Grant always being inclined to conceal his extensive reading. Both skilful writers, they could express themselves lucidly and concisely. Grant co-ordinated operations over much greater distances than did Moltke, though he never brought a quarter of a million men to a battlefield as the latter did. On the other hand, the calibre of the generals facing Grant was consistently higher than those defeated by Moltke – especially in 1864–5 when he eventually defeated Lee. Perhaps the secret of their success was that both shared an instinctive understanding of what was crucial in the higher direction of armies, and did not waste their energies on the insignificant or on detail. They both deprecated fixed 'laws' of war and relied on surprise and flexibility. Grant was the better logistician of the two. In 1864 Grant gave the Army of the Potomac forty wagons per thousand men, and never advanced more than ten miles per day for more than five days. Moltke would have considered such provision luxurious. Grant's attention to logistics has more to do with the nature of the campaign in which he was engaged rather than anything to do with the higher standard of living

1 29 August: Prussian manoeuvres force French commanded by MacMahon to fall back towards the border fortress of Sedan

2 1 September: Prussian forces under the command of Moltke surround the French Army and begin an artillery bombardment of the town

3 Afternoon: the French forces attempt a break out. After a violent fight they are forced back into Sedan, losing some 17,000 casualties and 20,000 prisoners

4 2 September: Napoleon decides to surrender. The surviving 83,000 French troops march out into captivity

prevailing in the United States in the 1860s. Grant waged an attritional campaign and Moltke did not, and he had to ensure that his men were contented before the fighting began.

Bazaine made two weak efforts to break out from Metz on 26 and 31 August. Moltke had been allowed to assemble a superior force at every important point and successfully kept the French armies apart. The only way that MacMahon could have defended Sedan successfully was by holding the high ground around the town, but, unsupported by Bazaine, he was too weak to do anything but withdraw into its streets.

FALL OF SEDAN

French defeat in 1870 was caused primarily by the failure to co-ordinate the two field armies, the Army of Châlons and the Army of the Rhine. Once the latter had withdrawn to Metz, the former was pushed back to Sedan. As soon as the Prussians had occupied the high ground around Sedan, which lies in a bowl on the banks of the Meuse with the Ardennes to the north, capitulation was likely. Break-out efforts were badly co-ordinated and thrown back in confusion. Fortune no longer smiled on the French Army.

Once the French had been driven back into Sedan its capitulation was only a matter of time. General Ducrot realized this as soon as he saw the encircling Prussian night camp fires. 'We are in a chamber pot, and now we will be shat upon,' he said mordantly. Once the encirclement was complete, Moltke began the bombardment of the town; there were no suicidal infantry charges as at St Privat. MacMahon was wounded and an unedifying squabble over who should succeed him led to a muddled attempt at break-out culminating in the ill-fated charge of the *Chasseurs d'Afrique* at Floing. This failure underlined the message that all battlefields were transmitting, namely, that cavalry as an offensive arm was too weak to bring decisive results when sent against well-equipped infantry supported by artillery. Sedan was surrendered on 2 September 1870 and offered up not only the imperial person of Napoleon III himself, but 83,000 prisoners in addition to the 21,000 taken during the battle, 413 field guns and 139 fortress guns. The surrender of Metz that followed in October freed a further seven corps that had been besieging the fortress town, and Moltke could concentrate his forces to reduce Paris itself. Prussian strength for this operation had risen to 630,736 men, 1,742 guns and 61,000 cavalry. Moltke could, moreover, use the efficient French railways to move and supply his besieging armies.

The twin disasters at Metz and Sedan signalled the collapse of the Second Empire and the foundation of the Third Republic that survived until 1940. It also ushered in a new, more determined phase of the war, as the revival of democracy in France inspired a resuscitation of national resistance to the invader. As the Prussians encircled Paris, Léon Gambetta took off in a balloon to raise new armies of National Defence in the south and west to replace the defeated imperial armies. For all their enthusiasm they did not make much impression on Moltke's successful forces. They were to mark a turning point in French military policy, however, and identify French republican values with universal military service, an idea which has lasted intact until very recent times. The *franc-tireurs*, or guerrillas, sprung up along Moltke's lines of operations and harassed his rear areas. Like those of

Sedan after the surrender of Napoleon III and the Army of Châlons in September 1870. The Prussians are assembling some of the huge quantities of captured war materials in front of the massive chateau in the centre of the town.

General John Pope in July 1862, Moltke's troops were ordered to shoot civilians and destroy houses used by snipers. This lightning war revealed a brutal phase that was not brought to an end until the fall of Paris in 1871. Until then the siege operations were slow and methodical and relied on starvation; Moltke brought up his big guns and bombarded the city, but they did not have a decisive effect until the garrison (and the citizens) were on the brink of starvation. As the siege came to an end, Moltke and Bismarck became involved in an acrimonious dispute over the extent to which punitive measures should be imposed on France, with Bismarck taking the more lenient view. In the event, the armistice

and the declaration, in the Hall of Mirrors at Versailles, of the king of Prussia as German Emperor were humiliating enough. By the Treaty of Frankfurt (1871), France was required to pay a massive indemnity of 5 billion francs and was stripped of Alsace and two thirds of Lorraine. Despite Bismarck's manipulations, this remained a grievance in great power relations that would disfigure the European scene until the issue was finally settled in 1914–18. Germany was to learn what the United States had learnt in 1865–77 when its army policed the Southern states, namely that statecraft and war cannot alter a people's attitudes when they are determined on a particular course.

Porte Maillot after the end of the siege and the suppression of the Commune which had reduced France to the brink of civil war. The leaders of the Third Republic were determined to eradicate the Commune, and did not shrink from killing on a large scale and applying martial law 'in all its rigour'.

Afterword

I N MAY 1890, during a speech before the Reichstag, Helmuth von Moltke declared, 'The age of cabinet war is behind us – now we only have people's war.' What Moltke had in mind by the term 'cabinet wars' was the wars he himself had fought: short, limited conflicts fought largely for territorial objectives which were easily satisfied; once the odd province was exchanged then peace would return. Only towards the end of the Franco-Prussian War did Moltke face the dilemmas of a people's war – when the passions of the masses were engaged and the aims of the conflict were enlarged accordingly, often embellished with emotion as the cost of victory rose. The Crimean War is significant in indicating the direction that the technique of war would henceforth take. The Franco-Prussian War reveals the degree to which organization improves a state's capacity for war. But it is the American Civil War, marked by a conspicuous lack of technique and organization at its outbreak – that signals the increasing social dimension accorded to warfare by the Industrial Revolution.

The North lacked a large enough military structure to defeat the South quickly, and failed to evolve an efficient enough organizational system to mobilize its manpower. Similarly, the fighting power that was gradually harnessed contributed to an indecisive conflict with much higher aggregate casualties than even the most gloomy of Cassandras might have predicted in 1861. As frustration grew and the costs mounted, so the war aims widened to embrace an attack on the very social system of the South – the destruction of slavery. To preserve the Union, Abraham Lincoln was forced reluctantly to take more severe measures; an act of preservation involved destruction, and the number of politicians and generals who not only sanctioned this step but greeted it enthusiastically increased as the war continued and the casualties piled up. If the Civil War had been fought in the 1990s, then as a proportion of today's population, five million Americans would have been killed. In adopting ambitious war aims and fighting to the finish – to ensure the complete military defeat of the Confederacy – the North became involved in an attritional conflict in which numbers and material counted for more than skill. Consequently, as in 1914–18 and in 1939–45, victory went to the side with the largest population, the most durable financial system and the greatest industrial capacity.

Clearly, in such a war strategy was aimed just as much at civilians as at enemy soldiers. In the Civil War it was Southern property that was the main target, though many civilians were killed. This was the result of a sober calculation: such a military effort would demonstrate to the Southern populace that the Confederacy was, to use Sherman's phrase, 'an empty shell' and lacked all moral credibility, let alone legitimacy, to call itself a nation state charged with their protection. The Union aimed at a psychological war, hoping to persuade Southerners to withdraw their support for the Confederacy. As General Sheridan claimed: 'reduction to poverty brings prayers for peace more surely and more quickly than does the destruction of human life'. In 1870, during the Siege of Paris, he urged Moltke to take similar action, so that French civilians should be left with 'nothing but their eyes to weep with'. James M. McPherson, the premier historian of the Civil War, calls this brutal approach to conflict 'remorseless war'.

Moltke found it unnecessary to take such a drastic step in 1871 because France was keen to end the Franco-Prussian War, not out of fear of what Moltke might do, but because of the danger that if the war continued it would lead to a social revolution and a rising of the left. And indeed the French premier, Adolph Thiers, suppressed the Paris Commune with a vigour that would have passed even the demanding standards set by General Sheridan. A similar fear had speeded up the termination of the Civil War in 1865, as conservative Confederate commanders, like Lee and Johnston, were keen to end it before the regular armies dissolved and more radical, guerrilla groups took Southern leadership out of their hands.

Of course there are other aspects of the conflict that deserve the much coined sobriquet, 'the first of the modern wars' (actually

popularized by Major General J. F. C. Fuller). Most notably, the role
of newspapers, popular opinion, propaganda and all the pressures
that can be brought to bear on a democracy involved in a protracted
war. This social dimension – a democratization of war – was
apparent in the Crimean War, and made itself felt in France after the
fall of the Second Empire, but its impact in the American Civil War
was much more significant. The American conflict was a *civil* war,
and the United States was a political democracy. None the less, the
scale of the Civil War, truly a war of mass involvement in every sense,
differentiates it from the other wars of this period. The Civil War was
also a war of mass production with distribution units to match. The
Quartermaster General of the Union Army, Montgomery C. Meigs,
presided over a wartime budget of $1.5 billion. Not only did he create
economies of scale for the purchase of camp equipment and tents but
also for uniforms and boots. It was his efforts that led to the
introduction of standard sizes for apparel and footwear that has had
such a profound effect on people's daily lives ever since 1865.

On the battlefield the pattern was more evolutionary than
revolutionary. The rifled musket did not effect a complete
transformation in tactics as was once claimed, because American
soldiers still stood and fired in volleys. None the less, the increase in
firepower can hardly be ignored, and contributed to an increased
indecisiveness of battle unless an army was commanded by an
exceptional man. The United States staff system, however, tended to
produce soldiers, such as McClellan, Buell and Rosecrans (and on the
Southern side Johnston and Bragg), who excelled as logisticians but
lacked confidence and imagination operationally. Furthermore, for all
their organizational skills, soldiers like McClellan failed to
understand that they had to be just as innovative in command and
staff work as in the equipment and support of their armies. In this
area American armies tended to lag behind – a weakness accentuated
perhaps by the curious anomaly that, despite the huge scale of
American Civil War operations, the average size of the armies

engaged was smaller than that commanded by the Duke of Wellington in the last phase of the Peninsular War in 1813–14.

Curiously, despite the attention given in this book to structural change inspired by the mass production methods of the Industrial Revolution, the importance of the personal factor in the conduct of war was, if anything, enhanced by the increase in the scale of warfare. The enlarged span of command demanded not only a greater intelligence-gathering capacity, but more precise, clear orders, and a tighter intellectual grip by the commander on the actual conduct of operations. Grant, Sherman, Lee and Moltke were not warriors of the MacMahon or Hooker variety – courageous showmen; but these generals, by their unobtrusive presence, dominated their operations more effectively than men of the Bazaine stamp. The more spread out operations became, the thicker the 'fog of war' billows up. 'Ignorance is the parent of fear,' Herman Melville warns us in *Moby-Dick* (1851). Yet, consistently, the role of cavalry as intelligence-gatherers was neglected in all the wars covered by this book, resulting in a significant increase in the number of meeting engagements incurred. These, in turn, made great moral demands on the flexibility of commanders.

For a host of reasons, then, all the wars covered in this book to some degree deserve the label 'modern'. They include some, but by no means all, of the characteristics that we associate with the two World Wars of the first half of the twentieth century. However, care must be used in employing such a term. Warfare since 1945 appears to be changing its character. Gone are organized fronts and clearly demarcated campaigns of the period 1850–1950. War now runs on for decades, often resulting in social disintegration and anarchy. Conflicts in Africa show that wars do not need industrial economies to be fought ferociously. Whether the American Civil War was a 'total war' or not is a subject of vociferous debate among historians. Perhaps the question need no longer be asked. For it could be argued that the American Civil War inaugurated a system of warfare that, among the sophisticated, industrialized powers, has run its course.

Biographies

CARDIGAN, 7TH EARL (1797–1868)

Born in Hambleden, Buckinghamshire, he entered the Army in 1824. By purchasing commissions he commanded the 15th Hussars (1832–3) and the 11th Hussars (1836–47). He led the change of the Light Brigade but considered it 'no part of a general's duty to fight the enemy among private soldiers'. Disputatious and belligerent to a remarkable degree, he ended his career as Inspector-General of Cavalry (1855–60). The woollen 'cardigan' is named after him.

LUCAN, 3RD EARL (1800–88)

He accompanied the Russians as a volunteer in the war against the Turks (1828). He succeded to the earldom in 1839. As commander of the cavalry in the Crimea, he became unpopular because of his justifiable caution in expending it in pointless skirmishes. He was promoted field marshal in 1887 shortly before his death.

ALEXANDER MENSHIKOV, PRINCE (1787–1869)

He was impulsive, and as Russian commander in the Crimea, simultaneously complacent. He placed too much faith in his numerical superiority and geographical advantages. At the Alma he invited 30 young ladies to enjoy a picnic on what he thought was an impregnable position. Yet his defence of Sevastopol was stubborn and imaginative.

RAGLAN, 1ST BARON (1788–1855)

A younger son of the Duke of Beaufort, he joined the Army in 1804 and served as the Duke of Wellington's military secretary in the Peninsula and at Waterloo, where he lost an arm. He was Tory MP for Truro, and in 1852 was raised to the peerage and appointed Master General of the Ordnance. In 1854 he was appointed C-in-C of the Crimean expedition. He had spent forty years behind a desk but there was no one better to take his place. He gave his name to the 'Raglan sleeve'.

Franz Edward Ivanovich Totleben (1818–84)

A brilliant engineer whose plans did much to frustrate Allied efforts during the siege of Sevastopol. He joined the Russian Army in 1836 and served in the Caucasus (1848–9). He arrived in Sevastopol in August 1854 and strengthened its defences by digging earthworks and exploiting fields of fire.

American Civil War

*USMA = United States Military Academy, West Point

General Braxton Bragg (1817–76, USMA* 1837)

Born in Warrenton, NC, Bragg was a commander whose reputation had been made at the Battle of Buena Vista, when General Zachary Taylor had urged him to give the Mexicans, 'A little more grape, Captain Bragg'. In 1862 he replaced Beauregard as Commander of the Army of Tennessee, but his qualities as an organizer were negated by his cantankerous nature. His many defeats gave him an unjustified reputation for incompetence; yet he lacked confidence as a tactician. In 1864 he served Jefferson Davis as military adviser.

Major-General Ambrose E. Burnside (1824–81, USMA 1847)

A gunner, Burnside's military experience before 1861 amounted to garrison duty in Mexico. In 1853 he resigned his commission and engaged in manufacturing repeating rifles and in railroad construction. He was a friend of both Lincoln and McClellan and his connections rather than his talent were responsible for his advancement. Defeated at Fredericksburg in December 1862, he commanded the Department of the Ohio and then IX Corps in the Virginia Campaign of 1864–5 until his resignation under a cloud in April 1865. Thereafter he held several railroad directorships and was elected three times to the Governorship of Rhode Island as a Republican (1866, 1867, 1868) and in 1874 to the Senate.

JEFFERSON DAVIS, PRESIDENT OF THE CONFEDERACY (1808–89, USMA 1828)
Born in Kentucky, he was brought up by an older brother. He graduated from
West Point and served in the Infantry. He entered Congress for Mississippi in
1845, but stood down to serve as a volunteer officer in the Mexican War. Davis
was Secretary of War in the Pierce administration (1853–7). Elected to the
Senate, he resigned in 1861 and stood as the unopposed candidate for the
Confederate presidency. Davis himself would have preferred to have been an
army commander.

MAJOR-GENERAL WILLIAM B. FRANKLIN (1863–1903, USMA 1843)
Franklin served with distinction in the Mexican War and in 1861 was in charge
of the construction of the Capitol dome. He was a protégé of McClellan and
a reasonably successful division and corps commander. He was blamed by
Burnside and McClellan's enemies for the defeat at Fredericksburg in
December 1862 and his career was ruined. Lincoln refused to cashier him but
he never returned to his former position and status, although he commanded
XIX Corps in the Red River campaign. After 1865 he became general manager
of Colt's Fire Arms Company and a Democratic presidential elector for
Samuel J. Tilden in 1876.

MAJOR-GENERAL JAMES A. GARFIELD (1831–81)
Of pioneer stock, Garfield worked as a schoolmaster before his election to the
Ohio Senate in 1859. Chief of staff of the Army of the Cumberland in
1862–3, Garfield's military career was marked by a readiness to learn and read
military manuals rare in volunteer generals. His promotion to major-general
occurred at the same time as his election to the House of Representatives, in
which he served nine times for Ohio. He was not a supporter of Grant, whom
he sensed as a political rival, and was one of the few Congressional voices who
voted against Grant's promotion to lieutenant general. Elected 20th President
in 1880, he was assassinated in 1881.

GENERAL ULYSSES S. GRANT (1822–85, USMA 1843)

Grant's boredom with the tedious routines of peacetime soldiering and resulting drinking problems stifled a promising career and he resigned in 1854. Everything he turned his hand to failed and he was rescued from obscurity by the patronage of Congressman Elihu B. Washburne, who was thereafter his political mentor. Grant was one of those rare men who realize their full potential in war. The higher he was promoted the better a general he became. Nicknamed 'Unconditional Surrender' after the fall of Fort Donelson in February 1862, Grant's career was controversial but successful, winning at Shiloh, Vicksburg, and Chattanooga. In March 1864 he was appointed general-in-chief, and personally directed the operations against Lee that culminated in his surrender at Appomattox in 1865. Casual in dress, slightly unkempt, Grant's unprepossessing appearance led many of his contemporaries to underrate him. Later writers came to view him as a quintessentially 'American' figure. His *Personal Memoirs* (2 vols, 1885–6) forms one of the classics of military literature.

MAJOR-GENERAL HENRY W. HALLECK (1815–72, USMA 1839)

He was author of *Report on the Means of National Defence* (1845) and *Elements of Military Art and Science* (1847). Regularly promoted, Halleck resigned in 1854 and headed a leading Californian law firm, Halleck, Peachey and Billings, with which he made a fortune. After presiding over the early victories in the West, Halleck was called to Washington as general-in-chief in July 1862. Once he had arrived in the East his reputation took a turn for the worse: his nickname 'Old Brains' changed to old 'Wooden Head'. During the re-shuffle of March 1864 he became Chief of Staff, a position in which he gained little lustre. Actually, he made a major contribution to organizing the Union victory.

MAJOR-GENERAL JOSEPH HOOKER (1814–79, USMA 1837)

In Mexico Hooker won all brevets for gallantry and meritorious service, a record unsurpassed by any lieutenant in the service. After resigning in 1853 he eked out a living by farming in California and Oregon. An able subordinate general capable at the Corps level, he was too unsteady for high command and resigned again in 1864 when (after his transfer to the West and success at Chattanooga), Sherman preferred his subordinate, James B. McPherson, to command the Army of Tennessee.

LIEUTENANT GENERAL THOMAS J. 'STONEWALL' JACKSON (1824–63, USMA 1846)

Jackson was the leading representative of mountainous Western Virginia in Lee's army. He was not a successful peacetime soldier, being too eccentric, disorganized and unkempt. In 1852 he resigned to become an instructor at the Virginia Military Institute. Like Grant, Jackson came alive in war and showed a steely resolve, inner strength and harsh ruthlessness that had been concealed by cosy peacetime routines. A superb corps commander, his generalship displayed the essential qualities of manoeuvre warfare as laid down by Jackson himself: 'Always mystify, mislead and surprise.'

GENERAL ALBERT SIDNEY JOHNSTON (1803–62, USMA 1826)

By comparison with his first promise, magnificent carriage and impressive looks, Johnston's pre-1861 career was rather anti-climactic. He had served in Texas's War of Independence and as the independent republic's Secretary of War (1838–40). Re-appointed to the US Army in 1849, he successively commanded the 2nd Cavalry (1855), the Department of Texas (1856–58), leading an expedition against the Utah Mormons, 1857), and the Department of Utah (1858–61). He commanded the Confederate Department of the West (No.2) thereafter, and although much criticized for indecision, Johnston showed that he had the moral qualities necessary for success as a commander before his sudden (and avoidable) death at Shiloh in April 1862.

GENERAL ROBERT E. LEE (1807–70, USMA 1829)

The archetypal Virginian gentleman, Lee was commissioned into the Engineers and distinguished himself in the Mexican War, serving on the staff of Winfield Scott. In April 1861 he was offered command of Union forces but he resigned his commission and organized the military forces of Virginia. Until June 1862 he served as Jefferson Davis's military adviser, and thereafter commanded the Army of Northern Virginia in an amazing series of victories. Lee's generalship and his inspiring example did much to foster Confederate nationalism, and help explain why the Confederacy lasted for four years rather than one.

LIEUTENANT GENERAL JAMES LONGSTREET (1821–1904, USMA 1842)
A shrewd tactician, Longstreet provided the stolid foundation in the Army of Northern Virginia for Jackson's lightning manoeuvres. Lee called him 'my Old War Horse', and Longstreet was particularly adept at the set-piece battle. He became increasingly opinionated and the transfer of his Corps to the Army of Tennessee led to a serious quarrel with Bragg. He was wounded at the Battle of the Wilderness but returned to his Corps for the final campaign in 1865. After Appomatox he was treated as a traitor because he joined the Republican Party.

MAJOR-GENERAL GEORGE B. MCCLELLAN (1826–85, USMA 1846)
Born in 1826 in Philadelphia of distinguished Connecticut ancestry, McClellan is at once the most fascinating and controversial of Civil War generals. He attended the University of Pennsylvania before going to West Point where he graduated second in his class. He served on the Military Commission which visited the Crimea in 1855. In 1857 he resigned to work on railroad engineering and by 1861 he was President of the Ohio and Mississippi Railroad. His military career got off to a sanguinary start in West Virginia but failed to live up to expectations. His campaigns in Virginia and Maryland in 1862 are marked by brilliance of strategic conception and mediocrity of tactical execution. Unsuccessful as the Democratic candidate for the presidency in 1864, he served as Governor of New Jersey 1878–81.

MAJOR-GENERAL IRVIN MCDOWELL (1818–85, USMA 1838)
McDowell taught tactics at West Point before his sponsor, Salmon P. Chase, helped him reach high command. In July 1861 under pressure from the newspapers McDowell put together a fine plan which came unstuck at First Manassas. He was replaced by McClellan, and served as a corps commander

during the Peninsular Campaign, although his troops were used to 'protect' Washington. He commanded III Corps in the Army of Virginia, but after Second Manassas became embroiled in the court-martial of Fitz-John Porter. He commanded the Department of the Pacific from July 1864. Solemn and humourless, a strict teetotaller, McDowell was not a dashing leader, but a competent administrator.

MAJOR-GENERAL GEORGE G. MEADE (1815–72, USMA 1835)

Meade was commissioned into the Corps of Topographical Engineers and served with distinction in the Mexican War. In the Virginia campaigns he served successively as brigade, divisional and corps commander, and gained in confidence, and in the respect with which he was held, at each level. His skill as an organizer of tactical movement became proverbial. Meade took command of the Army of the Potomac in the midst of the Gettysburg Campaign. During the battle, he demonstrated tactical skill in the defence but lacked enterprise. He served as army commander throughout the Virginia campaigns of 1864-65. He was self-effacing and rather lacking in confidence, and his frustrations worked themselves out in explosions of savage temper. He was known to his subordinates as 'Old Snapping Turtle'.

MAJOR-GENERAL MONTGOMERY C. MEIGS (1816–92, USMA 1836)

A graduate of the University of Pennsylvania and West Point, Meigs was a distinguished engineer, presiding over the extensions to Congress including the dome. In May 1861 he was appointed Quartermaster General of the Union Army. His record as logistical organizer was very impressive, disbursing funds of over a billion and a half dollars. He remained QMG until 1882. Meigs was an extremely efficient staff officer who prided himself on his puritanical rectitude. He yearned for a field command but his services were too valuable in Washington.

LIEUTENANT GENERAL LEONIDAS POLK (1806–1864, USMA 1827)

A room-mate of Jefferson Davis's at West Point, Polk resigned immediately after graduation to take holy orders and rose to become Missionary Bishop of the South West. He initially commanded the Western Department and the Army of Mississippi, which became absorbed as a corps into the Army of Tennessee. He detested Braxton Bragg, disobeyed or ignored orders, and feuded with his commander. For all his shortcomings, he was popular with the troops and was mourned by all except Bragg when he was killed at Pine Mountain in June 1864.

MAJOR-GENERAL JOHN POPE (1822–92, USMA 1842)

Pope was related to Mary Todd Lincoln by marriage, and took command of forces in the upper Mississippi river, seizing Island No. 10 in April 1862. But the apogee of Pope's military career arrived quickly and vanished just as rapidly. Appointed to command the Army of Virginia in June 1862, he was defeated at Second Manassas. Prone to bombast, he was disliked by McClellan's protégés. The latter was restored to command all forces in Virginia and Pope was sent to fight the Sioux Indians in the West, where he served creditably until his retirement in 1886.

MAJOR-GENERAL WILLIAM S. ROSECRANS (1819–1902, USMA 1842)

A competent organizer, imaginative strategist but poor tactician, Rosecrans's record 1862–3 was mixed. He had won only a defensive victory at Murfreesboro but had successfully occupied central Tennessee by the autumn of 1863. However, his reputation was shattered when he lost his head at Chickamauga, and he was relieved from command shortly thereafter. After the war he was appointed minister to Mexico, a position taken away from him in 1869 on Grant's elevation to the Presidency. In 1880 he was elected to the Senate as a Democrat and became Chairman of the Committee on Military Affairs until 1885.

LIEUTENANT GENERAL WINFIELD SCOTT (1786–1866)

General-in-chief of the US Army when the Civil War broke out, Scott was a Virginian of unimpeachable loyalty but astounding pomposity. He had served in the War of 1812 and had distinguished himself at Lundy's Lane (1814). The pinnacle of his military career occurred in 1847 during the Mexican War when he captured Mexico City by advancing from Vera Cruz. Well past his prime in 1861, he nonetheless expounded the attritional 'Anaconda Plan' which stressed advances in the Mississippi basin. He retired in November 1861.

GENERAL PHILIP H. SHERIDAN (1831–88, USMA 1853)

He was representative of the new breed of tough, dynamic and ruthless generals who came to the fore by 1864. Sheridan's rise was meteoric. His division fought stubbornly at Murfreesboro and had surged up Missionary Ridge. He caught Grant's attention and was appointed to command the cavalry of the Army of the Potomac. He defeated (and killed) Stuart at Yellow Tavern in May 1864. Showing phenomenal presence of mind, he crushed Early's Raid on Washington and then despoiled Shenandoah Valley so that 'a crow would be compelled to carry his own rations'. He played an important part in Lee's final surrender, with his victory at Five Forks, and by successfully blocking Lee's line of retreat from Richmond.

MAJOR-GENERAL DANIEL E. SICKLES (1819–1914)

A War Democrat from New York, Sickles was assigned to command New York's Excelsior Brigade, subsequently rising to command III Corps at Chancellorsville and Gettysburg, where he lost a leg. A confidant of both President and Mrs Lincoln, after the war he changed political colours to radical Republicanism, serving as military governor of South Carolina and later as US Minister to Spain, when he pursued a famous liaison with Queen Isabella.

EDWIN M. STANTON (1814–69)

Before 1861 Stanton had been a Democrat and had served in President James Buchanan's Cabinet, as Attorney-General. In 1862 he was appointed Secretary of War by Lincoln and soon veered towards favouring the radical Republican viewpoint, mainly because of his desire to win the war, and win it quickly. He was bad-tempered, devious and calculating, but not to the extent that some of his detractors have claimed. He was loyal, and eventually became closely attached to Lincoln. Stanton quickly realized (unlike other critics like Wade) Lincoln's true stature and abilities.

Major General J. E. B. Stuart (1833–64)

Affectionately known as 'Jeb', Stuart was a charming showman who embodied the chivalrous Southern cavalier, and he played up to the part with relish. But he was more than just a prancing peacock, and his handling of Lee's cavalry was marked by boldness and a keen eye. His reconnaissance services before May 1863 were outstanding. But he became protective of his reputation, and his efforts at embellishing it led to his absence for much of the Gettysburg Campaign. In 1864 his death at Yellow Tavern marked the beginning of the terminal decline of Confederate cavalry in the East.

Major-General Emory Upton (1839–81, USMA 1861)

Upton is important not so much for his military career, which was distinguished within limits, but for his writings, especially his posthumous *The Military Policy of the United States* (1907), which remained the standard work in the field until the 1950s. Upton took as his model the military system of Germany which embraced a large standing, regular army. Upton served with distinction in the Antietam, Fredericksburg, Chancellorsville, Spotsylvania and Shenendoah Valley campaigns. His record of jumping in rank from second lieutenant aged 21 to major-general by 26 has not been equalled. Gloomy but professionally dedicated, he committed suicide in 1881.

Major General Earl Van Dorn (1820–63, USMA 1842)

A typical cavalier, Van Dorn was colourful, careless in detail and an adventurer. He commanded the Army of the West in the Trans-Mississippi but lost the Battle of Pea Ridge in March 1862. Transferred to the Army of Mississippi, he was defeated at Corinth in October. His most notable achievement was the destruction of Grant's supply base at Holly Springs in December 1862. Van Dorn had a keen eye for the ladies (other men's wives were an especial attraction) and he was murdered by an outraged husband in May 1863.

BENJAMIN F. WADE (1800–78)

A Republican Senator from Ohio, Wade was born in New England in 1800. He moved to Ohio as a youth and engaged in various arduous tasks – including digging of canals – before winning acceptance as a clerk in the celebrated law practice of the anti-slavery leader Joshua R. Giddings. Wade was to hold his Senate seat after 1851 by denouncing the South's 'slave power'. He was considered by the future president, James A. Garfield, as 'a man of violent passions, extreme opinions and narrow views …' Courageous, impetuous, ruthless and outspoken, Wade was a dominant political figure in Washington as the Chairman of the Congressional Joint Committee on the Conduct of the War.

GERMAN WARS OF UNIFICATION

MARSHAL ACHILLE FRANCOIS BAZAINE (1811–88)

Born in Versailles but a resident of Lorraine, Bazaine was captured at Solferino (1859) and commanded the Mexican expedition, being promoted to Marshal of France in 1864. He was a reluctant commander of the Army of the Rhine, and in August 1870 managed to snatch defeat from the jaws of victory. After a siege of 54 days he surrendered Metz. Thereafter he was treated as a scapegoat, court martialled and imprisoned, but he escaped to Spain.

OTTO VON BISMARCK, PRINCE (1815–98)

He entered the Prussian parliament in 1847 and became known for his conservative, ultra-royalist views. Bismarck served as minister to St Petersburg and Paris before being recalled in 1862 to be foreign minister and then prime minister. The embodiment of *realpolitik*, Bismarck pursued the unification of Germany with cold, calculating ruthlessness. He liked wearing uniforms, eating large meals, and enjoyed an affectionate family life at odds with his cold public image.

MARSHAL MARIE EDMÉ MACMAHON, DUKE OF MAGENTA (1808–93)

A brave and outstanding leader, Macmahon (whose ancestors were among Louis XIV's 'Wild Geese' of exiled Irishmen) served in the Crimea and the Franco-Austrian War of 1859. In the Franco-Prussian War he was defeated at Wörth and surrendered Sedan, where he was wounded. In 1871 he suppressed the Paris Commune.

FIELD MARSHAL HELMUTH VON MOLTKE, GRAF VON (1800–91)

He was in born in Parchim, Prussia, and entered the Prussian Army in 1822. A profound student of military history and theory, he was a prolific writer. From 1858-88 he was Chief of the General Staff. His reorganization of the Prussian Army prepared the ground for his triumphs in 1864, 1866 and 1870–71. His exploitation of the general staff system transformed the ways in which armies are commanded and managed.

NAPOLEON III, EMPEROR OF THE FRENCH (1808–73)

He sought to bolster his shaky regime with military adventures: the Crimean War (1854–6), expeditions to China (1857–60), the Franco-Austrian War (1859) and the Mexican adventure (1861–7). His regime collapsed in 1870. By 1869–70 he was stricken with syphillis and kidney stone, and was heavily made up for public appearances. Visiting courtesans at the Tuileries Palace were instructed. 'You may touch His Majesty anywhere except on the face'.

Further reading

Among the liveliest and thought-provoking of all surveys of modern warfare is Major General J. F. C. Fuller, *The Conduct of War, 1789–1961* (1961; Methuen paperback). Hew Strachan, *European Armies and the Conduct of War* (1983; Unwin paperbacks) and Brian Bond, *War and Society in Europe, 1870–1970* (1984; reissued Alan Sutton, 1998) reflect more closely the preoccupations of modern scholars. Also of interest are the early chapters of Brian Bond, *The Pursuit of Victory: From Napoleon to Saddam Hussein* (Oxford University Press, 1996).

The causes of the wars studied in this book have been dealt with in Longmans's 'Origins of Modern Wars' Series (general editor Harry Hearder): David M. Goldfrank, *The Origins of the Crimean War* (Longman, 1994), William Carr, *The Origins of the German Wars of Unification* (Longman, 1991), and Brian Holden Reid, *The Origins of the American Civil War* (Addison Wesley Longman, 1996). The latter now effectively displaces the readable but dated and pro-Southern account by Avery O. Craven, *The Coming of the Civil War*, Second Revised Edition (1942; University of Chicago Press, 1957, 1973).

For the Crimean War, Hew Strachan, *Wellington's Legacy; The Reform of the British Army, 1830–54* (Manchester University Press, 1984) and *From Waterloo to Balaclava: Tactics, Technology and the British Army, 1815–54* (Cambridge University Press, 1985) sketch in the background. For France, see Paddy Griffith, *Military Thought in the French Army, 1815–51* (Manchester University Press, 1989). Andrew Lambert, *The Crimean War: British Grand Strategy Against Russia* (Manchester University Press, 1990) and Hew Strachan 'Soldiers, Strategy and Sebastopol', *Historical Journal*, vol XXI (1978), pp. 303–25, provide the essential strategic   foreground. Then for Balaclava, see The

Marquess of Anglesey, *A History of the British Cavalry, 1816–1919*, Vol II: *1851–1871* (1975; Leo Cooper, 1989). Christopher Hibbert, *The Destruction of Lord Raglan* (Longmans, 1961) is really a general history; John Sweetman, *Raglan* (Arms and Armour Press, 1993) is more clearly focused on its subject.

The literature on the American Civil War is huge. The starting point is Steven E. Woodworth (ed.), *The American Civil War: A Handbook of Literature and Research* (Greenwood Press, 1996) and Peter J. Parish (ed.), *The Reader's Guide to American History* (Fitzroy Dearborn, 1997). The best single volume accounts are by Peter J. Parish, *The American Civil War* (Eyre Methuen, 1975), James M. McPherson, *The Battle Cry of Freedom: The Civil War Era* (Oxford University Press, 1988) and James L. Stockesbury. *A Short History of the Civil War* (Morrow, 1995). Of military accounts, Herman Hattaway and Archer Jones, *How the North Won* (University of Illinois Press, 1984) and Edward Hagerman, *The American Civil War and the Origins of Modern Warfare* (Indiana University Press, 1988) are by far the best. Paddy Griffith, *Battle Tactics of the American Civil War* (Yale University Press, 1990) is contentious and provocative but too sweeping and prone to error.

On Northern strategy, T. Harry Williams, *Lincoln and his Generals* (Alfred A. Knopf, 1952) is a marvellous book that has worn remarkably well. Rowena Reed, *Combined Operations in the Civil War* (1978; University of Nebraska, Bison Books, 1993) offers a pro-McClellan view. On the debate over the reasons for the Confederate defeat, Richard E. Beringer, Herman Hattaway, Archer Jones and William N. Still, Jr, *Why the South Lost the Civil War* (University of Georgia Press, 1986) and Gary W. Gallagher, *The Confederate War* (Harvard University Press, 1997) offer contrasting explanations.

Much Civil War writing has been biographical in scope. Only a sample of the portraits of leading personalities can be recommended here. David Donald, *Lincoln* (Simon and Schuster, 1995), Stephen W. Sears, *The Young Napoleon: George B. McClellan* (Ticknor and Fields, 1988), Freeman Cleaves, *Meade of Gettysburg* (1960; University of Oklahoma Press, 1991), William S. McFeely, *Grant* (Norton, 1981), and John F. Marszalek, *Sherman: A Soldier's Passion for Order* (Free Press, 1993). Of Confederates, William C. Davis, *Jefferson Davis: The Man and the Hour* (Harper Collins, 1991), T. Harry Williams, *P. G. T. Beauregard: Napoleon in Gray* (1955; Louisiana State University Press, 1989), Emory M. Thomas, *Robert E. Lee* (Norton, 1995), and Craig L. Symonds, *Joseph E. Johnston* (Norton, 1992) are readable and authoritative.

Two books that illuminate general attitudes about the war are Marcus Cunliffe, *Soldiers and Civilians: The Martial Spirit in America, 1775–1865*, Third Edition (Gregg Revivals, 1993) and Mark Grimsley, *The Hard Hand of War* (Cambridge University Press, 1995).

On the Austro-Prussian War of 1866, see Gordon A. Craig, *The Battle of Königgrätz* (Weidenfeld and Nicolson, 1964), although Geoffrey Wawro, *The Austro-Prussian War* (Cambridge University Press, 1996) is now to be preferred because he considers the war in its full context. Michael Howard, *The Franco-Prussian War* (Rupert Hart-Davis, 1961) remains the unassailable standard work in English. Richard Holmes, *The Road to Sedan: The French Army, 1866–70* (Royal Historical Society, 1984) is important in explaining the French defeat, and Alistair Horne, *The Fall of Paris: The Siege and the Commune, 1870-71* (Macmillan, 1965) the aftermath.

There have been few attempts at drawing general conclusions about the wars of the mid-nineteenth century. A recent comparative enterprise is *On the Road to Total War: The American Civil War and the German*

Wars of Unification, 1861–1871 (eds.) Stig Förster and Jörg Nagler (Cambridge University Press, 1997). Philip Howes, *The Catalytic Wars: A Study of the Development of Warfare, 1860–1870* (Minerva Press, 1998) offers some perceptive points but his treatment is too diffuse. Jay Luvaas, *The Military Legacy of the Civil War* (1959; University of Kansas Press, 1989) considers the significance of the war for European military thought; so does Brian Holden Reid, *Studies in British Military Thought: Debates with Fuller and Liddell Hart* (University of Nebraska Press, 1998).

The 1st Baden Grenadier Regiment storms the railway embankment near Nuits (on the Côte d'Or) south of Dijon on 18 December 1870. The French soldiers surrendering (by holding their rifles upside down) are among the new regiments of Gardes Nationales *raised by Gambetta. Over 1,000 surrendered after this action.*

Index

Figures in *italic* refer to captions

Picture credits

Every effort has been made to contact the copyright holders for images reproduced in this book. The publishers would welcome any errors or omissions being brought to their attention.

Corbis-Bettmann: pp. 2, 18–19, 33, 77, 97, 103, 144–5, 147, 162, 176, 180–81; 30–31, 54, 75, 124, 150, 160, 172 UPI Corbis. AKG: pp. 21, 48, 87, 188, 190, 194, 198, 229. Mary Evans Picture Library: pp. 29, 38–9, 53, 59, 64–5. Hulton-Getty: pp. 35, 42, 68–9, 72, 102, 109, 121, 136, 164, 179, 182–3, 195, 199, 206–7, 208–9. Library of Congress: pp. 84, 106–7, 132. Brady Collection: 93, 153 Library of Congress; 148 National Archives. Chicago Historical Society: pp. 115, 155. War Department General Staff: pp. 128–9.

The drawings on pages 26 and 27 are by Peter Smith and Malcolm Swanston of Arcadia Editions.